ultralight BOATBUILDING

ultralight BOATBUILDING

THOMAS J. HILL

with Fred Stetson

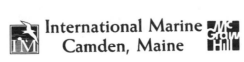

International Marine
Camden, Maine

Published by International Marine Publishing

10   9   8

Library of Congress Cataloging in Publication Data

Hill, Thomas J., 1954-
Ultralight boatbuilding.

Includes index.
1. Boatbuilding.   I. Stetson, Fred.   II. Title
VM351.H55   1987   623.8'223   87-17057

ISBN 0-87742-244-3

Questions regarding the ordering of this book should be addressed to:

The McGraw-Hill Companies
Customer Service Department
P.O. Box 547
Blacklick, OH 43004
Retail customers: 1-800-822-8158
Bookstores: 1-800-722-4726

Design by Janet Patterson
Illustrated by Elayne Sears
Photography by Michael Weizenegger
Production by Janet Robbins
Edited by Jonathan Eaton, Emily Boochever

The sail plan drawings on pages 119, 121, 122, 123 and 124 copyright Stephen Redmond.
Reprinted with permission.

To Carl Bausch

Contents

Acknowledgments

Building small boats is relatively easy. Building books is another matter. Without the help of many friends, this book would still be in dry dock. I'd like to thank Carl Bausch for sharing his insights about building canoes, Fred Stetson for the many months he spent helping me organize and write, and Jonathan Eaton for his patience and skill editing this book. Also, I thank Steve Redmond for reviewing the manuscript and sharing his fine skiff designs. Steve and I collaborated on prototypes for the Whisp, Flapjack, Tetra, and Bluegill. Michael Weizenegger deserves a Purple Heart for overcoming injury and taking technically accurate photographs of ultralight boatbuilding. Many thanks to Elayne Sears, who completed the beautiful illustrations on a tight deadline. For the past ten years, *WoodenBoat* magazine and The Wooden Boat School have been generous supporters. Thanks to my wife, Polly, for her support; her hard work paid our bills while this book was built.

Tom Hill

1
Glued Plywood Lapstrake Construction

I started building boats in the early 1970s, and I guess I've built about a hundred of them over the years. Yet each completed boat gives me the same thrill as the first one, the same deep satisfaction. The process itself—creating from lines drawn on sheets of paper an object that is not only beautiful but perfect for its intended use—is no less fascinating now than when I started. What has changed for me is the materials and methods with which I choose to build. My first boats were of traditional plank-on-frame construction, and I've since built with fiberglass, cedar-strip, and cold-molding methods. Once I started building ultralight boats, however, I realized that no other approach can produce such strong, good-looking boats so quickly and economically.

Ultralight boats are built of lightweight, high-quality, mahogany plywood planking, easy to shape yet dimensionally stable. It is also rigid, which means you can build a stiff, watertight hull. These are lapstrake boats; each plank overlaps the top edge of the one below, and the laps effectively double the thickness of the plywood and the number of laminations, creating tight, boat-length joints. Once bonded with a strong epoxy glue, each lap becomes a chine or stringer, adding strength and structural integrity.

The result is a hull in which the outer skin carries most of the stress. Because the boat is so rigid, you can minimize or eliminate framing, which reduces weight and fasteners. It also means less interior clutter, which simplifies the sanding, painting, and cleaning of the hull.

Ultralight canoes are ideally suited to flat-water paddling, where stiffness is a plus. The rigid hulls won't flex, or "oilcan." In some canoes made of synthetic materials, if you bounce on the seat, you can see the bottom flex up and down. That's great for white-water canoeing with a current pushing you over rocks, but when crossing a lake, you want stiffness in a boat. Flex causes turbulence and drag, which slows you down.

Lapstrake boats have been built for centuries, and plywood has been widely used for at least the past 50 years. In recent years, though, the quality of plywood and glue and the methods of construction have improved markedly, and acceptance of plywood among boatbuilders has increased. In a lapstrake boat built correctly with high-grade mahogany plywood and watertight epoxy, you need have no worries about leaks due to swelling and shrinking.

I prefer lightweight Bruynzeel mahogany plywood, which I consider simply the best-quality plywood I've ever seen. How durable is it? Lloyd's of London guarantees it for 20 years, a sure sign of confidence. In my home

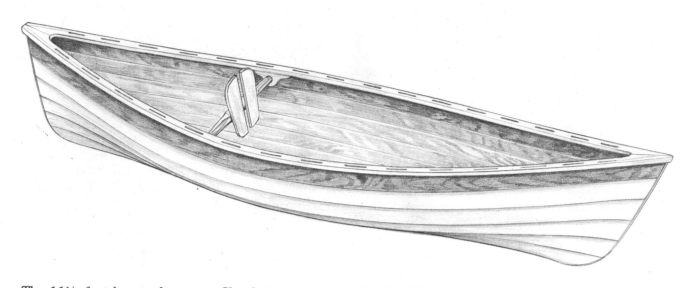

The 11½-foot lapstrake canoe Charlotte, one of two boatbuilding projects described step by step in the chapters ahead.

garden, I use discarded scraps as vegetable stakes. Season after season, they sit in the often-wet, muddy clay—the worst possible conditions. In the winter, snow covers them. After six years, there's not a hint of delamination.

Another story attests to this wood's endurance. Kenneth Mobert, a California boatbuilder, placed pieces of the plywood in a steam box alongside a piece of white oak. Then he applied heat to the box—10 hours a day for 10 straight days. After 100 hours, the oak fell apart but the plywood did not delaminate.*

For planking, I prefer a type of mahogany plywood called occume. While you can build a simple small boat with other species or with standard construction-grade plywood, I don't recommend it. For canoes, I buy 4-millimeter occume exclusively; for other small boats, I use 4- to 12-millimeter. Occume plywood holds up well when you plane across its end grain. Tear-outs, a common problem with fir plywood, seldom occur.

One of the beauties of ultralight boatbuilding is that you can order mahogany plywood and have it shipped anywhere in the country. To order Bruynzeel plywood, or a good substitute (or any other hard-to-find materials), refer to Appendix C. Mahogany plywood costs about twice as much as standard construction grades, but over the long run, it's worth the added expense.

Although the plywood is expensive, the building method is ultimately economical because you can "nest" curved planks on the panels, minimizing waste. Materials for a 12-foot canoe cost about $250, including paint and fasteners. More important, the method is economical in its demands on the builder's time and patience. Epoxy glue, for example, makes it easy for a first-time builder to turn out a watertight boat. On a warm summer day, I can hang three pairs of planks, or, in other words, both sides of a skiff. In the winter, when working in my northern Vermont boatshop, I warm the glue by the woodstove and warm the boat surfaces with a 4-foot electric baseboard heater. The work goes a little more slowly, but still much more rapidly than any other building method I've tried.

Wherever possible, I try to find ways to simplify the process still further. For example,

*Kenneth C. Mobert, "Plywood Lapstrake Construction," *WoodenBoat*, Number 43, pp. 44–49.

my low-angle block plane has a special guide that guarantees I'll cut perfect winding bevels on the planks every time (Chapter 7). The building jigs have precisely spaced ribbands (Chapter 4) that guide the plane and enable me to mark, cut, and bevel planks in quick, easy steps. I can bevel a plank on a 12-foot canoe in 3 minutes, and with a little practice,

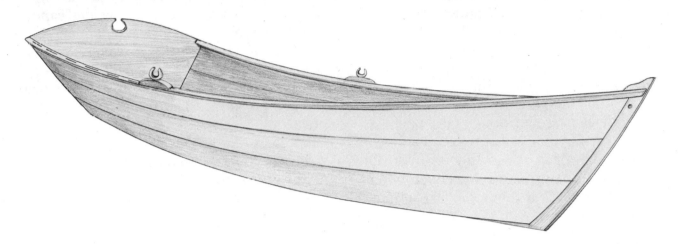

Flapjack, a 14-foot lapstrake skiff, is the other boat covered in this book. The building techniques described for Flapjack and Charlotte can be applied to a variety of small boats, canoes, and kayaks.

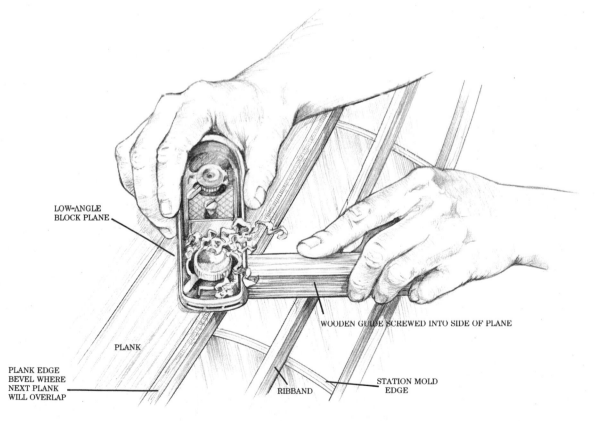

LOW-ANGLE
BLOCK PLANE

WOODEN GUIDE SCREWED INTO SIDE OF PLANE

PLANK

PLANK EDGE
BEVEL WHERE
NEXT PLANK
WILL OVERLAP

RIBBAND

STATION MOLD
EDGE

This simple modification of a plane enables you to make perfect plank bevels every time. By pressing the wooden guide down flush against the adjoining ribband as shown, you ensure that the bevel aligns with the top face of the ribband. The procedure is described in Chapter 7.

so can you. On the third day of my two-week summer boatbuilding courses, my students can hang a pair of planks in 2½ hours.

The point I'm trying to make is that ultralight boatbuilding is well within the grasp of anyone possessing a little patience, a few fairly basic tools, and a space big enough to build in. Large, stationary power tools, to give one example, are unnecessary.

While this book focuses on the building of two boats—a canoe and a sailing skiff—several other designs are introduced in Appendix B. Beyond these, you can adapt for glued plywood lapstrake construction almost any small boat that was designed originally for other lapstrake construction methods. The principles of lofting (Chapter 3) and jig building (Chapter 4) are unchanging.

Ultralight boats are proof that elegance and strength are not mutually exclusive. They have the look of fine yachts, yet they are simple beyond belief. A small, lightweight canoe can be placed on top of a car and launched in remote spots. Because it's so easy to transport, it will be used and enjoyed often. Upkeep on a frameless boat is easy, too: An entire canoe can be sanded and refinished in just 3 hours.

You can build an ultralight boat. I'm sure of it. I hope you find both the process and the result as rewarding as I have.

2
Tools and Workspace

When building an ultralight canoe or skiff, you don't need an elaborate shop. Even the term *shop* suggests more than what's required. All along the nation's coastal waters, craftsmen build oceangoing boats under simple shelters or outdoors. Tarps, sheds, outbuildings, lean-tos, garages, or cellars are all fine for small-boat building.

Summer or winter, polyethylene-covered shelters are inexpensive and popular. Many builders simply nail together a 2 x 4 framework over their boat, leaving enough room to work around the hull, and cover the frame with plastic. The point is, you can build an ultralight boat with little room and little experience. You need just three things—materials, space, and hand tools. Heavy duty, expensive, stationary power tools, such as planers, band saws, and table saws, though helpful, are not required. For workspace, the only requirement is a few feet more than the length and width of your chosen boat.

A well-organized workspace and sharp hand tools are essential. When you handle materials and use tools in an organized way, enjoyment and efficiency increase. For the most part, the necessary hand tools aren't expensive, and they don't require extensive previous experience.

A few of my tools have been designed or modified expressly for building ultralight boats with the methods I've developed. As we go along, I'll describe these tools in detail and identify the brands, models, and specific features I prefer. At the same time, however, I recognize that other tools are every bit as good, so don't be afraid to substitute. When discussing common tools such as hammers and squares, I'll limit my remarks to their specific applications for building ultralights.

When working with wood, I always prefer a cutting tool such as a plane or spokeshave over an abrasive tool such as a rasp or grinder. I keep my cutting tools sharp. As any woodworker or carpenter knows, dull tools lead to frustration. I have an old drawknife of my great grandfather's; when sharpened, its thin, laminated steel reflects like a mirror.

Nowadays, I often find that certain foreign-made cutting tools are among the best. I'm impressed by hand tools from Japan, a country known for its fine cutlery and joinery. I have an extremely thin Japanese backsaw that's almost dangerously sharp, but perfect for the kind of work I do. I sharpen my edge tools with Japanese waterstones.

The Well-Organized Shop

My 1,250-square-foot shop is bigger than necessary. In a typical day, I walk repeatedly up and down the floor. Thousands of times in the course of building 100 canoes and small boats I've reached for a saw, taken a template off the wall, plugged in a drill, cut a plank, lifted a jig, or ripped a piece of plywood. In any boat-production project, regardless of size, reducing

5

the number of steps is crucial. Even if you're only in it for fun, the more efficient you are, the more fun it becomes.

Workbench. To minimize steps, I've put my workbench in an optimum, close-to-central position. For the best possible lighting, I have the bench near the shop's south-facing windows but 4 feet from the walls. That way, I can work easily from all sides of the bench's hardwood surface. Three deep drawers and a wide lower shelf conveniently store almost all my essential hand tools, as well as hand-held power tools such as the circular saw, jigsaw, and drill.

Catwalk. I have covered the concrete floor immediately around the bench with inexpensive particle board, slightly elevated with well-spaced scrap strips. This springy catwalk keeps my feet off the cold concrete in the winter and reduces fatigue in my legs and lower back—no small consideration when you're working long hours handling tools and materials or bending over the bench vise to cut, shape, or sand a piece of your boat.

Sawhorses. At my back as I face the bench, and about 8 feet from the south wall, is a pair of 32-inch-high sawhorses on which I have fastened flat 2 x 4 crosspieces covered with carpet to support a building jig without scratching or movement. When building sawhorses, consider your jig dimensions (Chapter 4), your own height, and the desired level for comfortable work on the hull. I made a second pair of sawhorses with concave crosspieces for canoes and small boats with round hulls. (Carpet strips draped between sawhorses also work well.) These cradle the boats upright. In this position, the hull interior is accessible for painting, varnishing, or other finish work.

Boat Orientation. Throughout construction, the bow of any boat I build points toward the door, and the boat and jig remain parallel to the workbench. I find that the bow-to-the-door, parallel arrangement significantly re-duces confusion, especially when hanging planks on double-enders (Chapter 7).

Heat. A few feet from the jig and workbench, I have a barrel-shaped woodstove. I store combustibles such as paints and varnishes at the opposite end of the shop. In the winter, I move my epoxy nearer the heat source when it's time to warm it to an optimum temperature for easy application and best results.

Electricity. Even though you'll need an extension cord to operate hand-held power tools, the more electrical outlets you have, the better. With a convenient, nearby wall socket, you can make life easier for yourself in the winter. On cold days I place a 4-foot section of electric baseboard directly beneath my boat, mounted on the building jig. Then I carefully heat the plywood planks, warming them to ideal temperatures for the epoxy.

Consider the above as recommendations based on my experience, not as hard and fast rules. One summer, I taught a class of eight students in a striped wedding tent. The open air was perfect, especially for gluing, sanding, painting, and varnishing.

Hand Tools for Boatbuilders

Low-Angle Block Plane. This is my most-used tool, essential for building small boats. I use it, for example, when scarfing together 2-foot-wide plywood panels end-to-end to make planking stock (see Chapter 5). A scarf is made by beveling and then gluing two pieces, and the low-angle block plane makes short work of the beveling while seldom causing "tear-outs," or end damage to the plywood. More generally, this plane performs well anytime you must plane across the grain. (Another good beveling tool is the #78 Stanley rabbet plane with its bullnose attachment removed.)

I have modified my low-angle block plane with a special wood guide to enable me to

Align your boat parallel with and near your bench to minimize steps and help you maintain your spatial orientation as you walk planks back and forth between jig and workbench.

bevel planks easily while they're mounted on longitudinal ribbands on the building jig. As I push forward, the guide rests on ribbands that represent the next adjacent plank of the boat's hull, keeping the tool on track and allowing me to plane perfect winding bevels without fuss. The photograph on page 45 in Chapter 7 shows the guide in action.

Carl Bausch, a Vermont canoe builder, designed this ingenious guide. To make one, simply drill a small hole into one end of a 6-inch-long piece of 1 x 1 hardwood. Insert a piece of threaded bolt into the hardwood, then screw the bolt into the threaded hole on the side of the plane. If your plane does not have such a hole, you'll need to drill and tap one. (The #78 Stanley rabbet plane, for one, has a threaded hole provided.)

Jack Plane. My sturdy, well worn jack plane has the name "W.S. Thayer" on one side. I picked it up at a local flea market for $15. Longer and narrower than a smoothing plane, the jack plane is ideal for making edges straight. I often use mine to bevel the chines.

Spokeshaves. I have three different spokeshaves, and I use them all. As the name suggests, a spokeshave was once used for rounding square, narrow stock to the shapes of wagon- or carriage-wheel spokes. In boatbuilding, I use these tools to shave spars or to make fine cuts on intricate parts such as stems or thwarts.

I have two 9-inch-long spokeshaves with 1¾-inch irons, or blades, that can be adjusted for depth. One shave has a flat base, while the

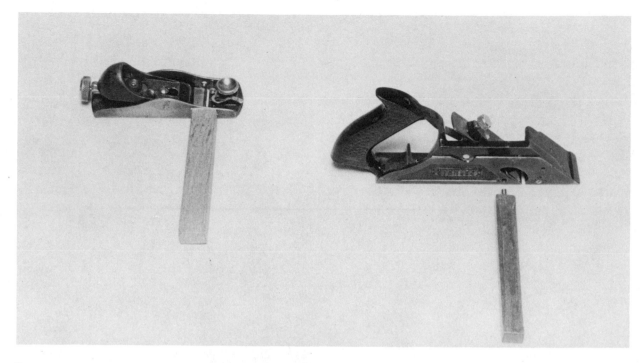

Low-angle block plane and Carl Bausch's rabbet plane, with wood guides, for beveling planks.

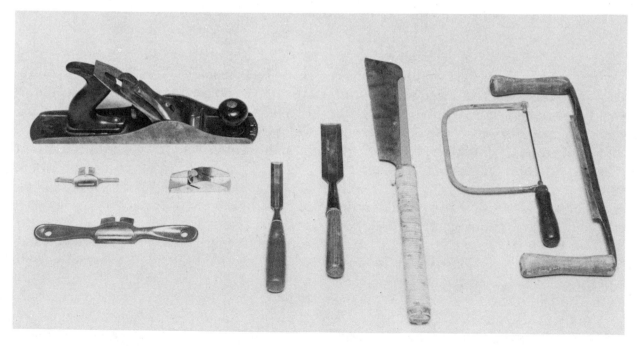

My cutting tools include the jack plane, spokeshaves, chisels, backsaw, coping saw, and drawknife. The spokeshaves and drawknife are not essential.

other is concave. I prefer the latter because it offers greater control and ease of cutting. My third spokeshave is 3½ inches long with a 1-inch iron.

With these shaves, especially the smaller one, you can cut accurately and quickly. The shave with the 1-inch blade is ideal for work in curves or tight spots such as the inside of a breasthook curve. With this tool, you can cut clean, well-defined surfaces—the kind that make for tight-fitting joints.

Chisels and Mallet. I own a range of chisels, with blades measuring ¼ to 1½ inches, suitable for building small boats. Sometimes, I drive a chisel with a mallet, covered on its striking face with leather. The leather softens blows to the chisel's wooden handle. Because a mallet has such a wide surface, it's a good striking tool to use when your eyes are focused elsewhere. You can hit the end of your chisel properly and easily while concentrating on a difficult cut.

Drawknife. I use my drawknife for only a few specific tasks—for example, roughing out stock for the stem. With a drawknife, you can remove a lot of wood in little time, but it takes more skill than a spokeshave, because the angle and depth of the cut are determined by the user, not by the setting of the iron. You, the craftsman, control how much wood you take in each bite. Pay attention to grain direction so that you don't take too much. The photograph on page 107, Chapter 9, shows a drawknife in action.

Handsaw. Even though I have a band saw, there are times when my standard 26-inch crosscut saw comes in handy. If the band saw is unplugged or if it's winding down, I can grab the handsaw and make a quick and quiet crosscut. Also, handsaws don't shoot splinters into your eyes.

Coping Saw. This saw is excellent for trimming or cutting curves in the thin, 4-millimeter plywood panels I use for planking. If a piece of planking hangs proud—off the end of the stem, for example—I can use this saw to trim the plank to make its edge conform with the curve of the stem.

When I set up the coping saw, I install the blade so that it cuts on the pull. Most Western saws, including my 26-inch handsaw, cut on the push, but I think it's easier and more effective to cut as you're pulling the tool. This way, also, the cutting action matches that of my Japanese saw, which cuts on the pull.

Japanese Backsaw. This is an extremely sharp saw with a reinforced back and a blade no thicker than the cover of a tuna can. The sharp blade with rigid teeth makes for fast, accurate cutting. With this saw, I can cut about three times faster than I can with any of my Western saws. For ultralight boats the Japanese backsaw is particularly useful for cutting the gains in the plank ends. Chapter 8 discusses these cuts and shows the saw in use.

While I recommend these saws, they require care. If you nick yourself with a Western saw, you might get a scrape or a shallow cut. If you run a Japanese backsaw over your hand, you're in for a deep wound.

Electrically Powered Hand Tools

Skilsaw. An excellent, electrically powered hand tool for cutting wood is a Model 77 Skilsaw. This is a powerful, quick-action saw that is both comfortable and safe to use. Unlike those of many circular saws, the Model 77 blade is on the left-hand side of the machine. This permits you to see better and therefore make more accurate cuts. Without straining to look over your work or the machine, you can actually see the blade. Also, the blade doesn't spit sawdust in your way—right where you want to look.

Some conventional circular saws have cumbersome mechanisms for adjusting the blade depth. On some, for example, a knob or perhaps two knobs must be loosened and then

Hand-held power tools include a jigsaw, drill, 4 X 4 sander, circular saw, and laminate trimmer.

tightened to make this adjustment. The Model 77 Skilsaw, on the other hand, has a quick-action cam. One movement of a lever operates the cam, adjusting the blade to the needed depth.

Another good feature of the Model 77 Skilsaw is the location of the handle and trigger—at the back of the saw, rather than at the top. In the top position, the operator must lean up and over the saw to hold the handle and see the work before him. With the handle at the back of the saw, you can stand slightly back, in a position that's more comfortable and natural.

Jigsaw. When building canoes and skiffs, this is the essential tool for cutting planks from thin, lightweight plywood. No other tool does the job as well.

I've used several different jigsaws for both boatbuilding and carpentry work, but I prefer the Hitachi four-position hand-held saw. The four settings produce different speeds and blade actions. In the position I favor, the blade moves fore and aft as well as up and down.

With the Hitachi jigsaw equipped with a fine-toothed metal-cutting blade, I find I get very few tear-outs. I can cut closer to a line than I would with the Skilsaw—and I'll feel comfortable when making the cut.

Laminate Trimmer. An electrically powered laminate trimmer is nice to have, but not essential. I use mine primarily for trimming planks flush to the ribbands when the planks are on the building jig. Either a router or a small Stanley trimming plane would do as well.

Variable-Speed Drill. My variable-speed, 3/8-inch drill, made by Makita, operates both forward and in reverse. Other drills work just as well. I once owned a one-direction drill that I bought for $12. It lasted about six years—and that's a lot of holes for $12. I use my Makita for countersinking and driving the few screws I use in my canoes and skiffs. For example, while the glue is drying, I use screws to hold planks to the stem and transom.

I also have a series of number 6 through 14 Fuller countersinks and accompanying "plug cutters." As their name suggests, these cut out small plugs that are later reinserted once a screw is in place. I prefer those with four "knives," or cutting blades, because they're more effective than plug cutters with just two.

Sander. An electrically powered sander is not absolutely essential for boatbuilding. You can sand by hand, but my feeling is—who wants to? I've used both Hitachi and Makita 4 x 4 vibrator sanders. Either one works well.

Beading Tool. There are many ways to add a distinctive, decorative bead to the edge of wood. One of the most ingenious tools I own is a small beading tool that cuts a bead in my rails with the edge of a screw. My friend Kenneth Steinmetz designed it.

To make a beading tool, simply drive a number 6 flathead steel wood screw into the edge of a 3/4-inch-thick disk of hardwood. Shape the disk so that it's about 1 1/2 inches in diameter. To sharpen the screw for precise beading, file it flat across the head.

As an example of how this tool works, let's say you've built a handsome canoe and, as a finishing touch, would like to carve a bead (an ornate groove) along the gunwale near its bottom edge. With the canoe right side up, hold the top surface of the disk firmly flush against the bottom of the gunwale. Rotate the disk until the screw contacts the outside edge of the gunwale, perhaps 1/8 or 3/16 inch up from the bottom (back the screw into or out of the disk to adjust this height). Now run the disk along the gunwale and let the screw head

Miscellaneous Tools

Marine Epoxy. Many good marine glues are available, but the one I've found most successful for glued plywood lapstrake construction is West System 105 Epoxy Resin, made by Gougeon Brothers. You can buy this high-grade marine epoxy in various quantities. A one-gallon can is enough to complete a small boat. Along with the glue, I buy two inexpensive plastic minipumps. These screw into the caps of the cans and allow you to dispense precise amounts of glue and hardener. Depending on the climatic conditions, I mix the glue with West System 205 Fast Epoxy Hardener or West System 206 Slow Epoxy Hardener. I also mix the glue with microballoons to create a filler putty. I apply the glue with plumber's acid brushes or putty knives. Most of these materials, application instructions, and gloves are available from Gougeon Brothers (for the address, see Appendix C).

A simple hand-operated tool for cutting beads on rails. The sharp edge of the screw head does the cutting, and the groove in the screw allows shavings to exit.

scribe a starting groove for the bead. Return to the starting point for another pass, this time rotating the screw more firmly into the gunwale. As you work, the shavings will squirt neatly out of the screw slot. One big advantage of this tool is that you can bead wood in place on your boat. With a shaper or router, beading must usually be done before installing a piece.

Scrapers. When working with glues, paints, and varnishes, scrapers are handy tools to have. One of my favorites is a putty knife whose blade I shortened by grinding and sharpening. The shorter blade is more rigid and therefore more effective for filling and removing excess glue. I sharpen the blade at a slight angle to facilitate scraping and glue removal.

I have a second tool, a 2- by 6-inch piece of flat steel, for scraping flat surfaces. For such jobs as reconditioning the top of my workbench, it's ideal. When pushing the steel back and forth, I hold it firmly between my thumbs and fingers at a 45-degree angle. When it is sharp, the scraper works like a plane, taking thin shavings off a surface.

Rasps and Sanders. Although I prefer cutting to abrasive tools, I do have two rasps and one 2½- by 4-inch sanding block for tight, hard-to-reach spots. I glue a small piece of old carpet or foam-rubber sheet on the block's surface to make the sandpaper more effective on contour surfaces.

I prefer Nicholson rasps with randomly cut teeth; those with straight-cut teeth do not cut as easily, quickly, or efficiently. My rasp has a 10-inch-long blade and can be purchased at almost any hardware store.

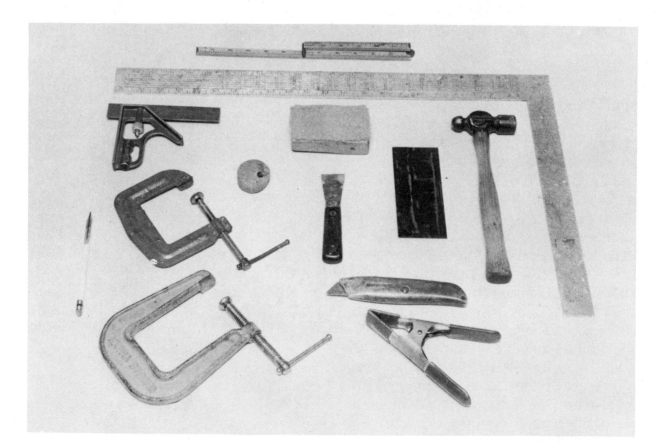

Miscellaneous tools include the 2-foot folding rule, 2-foot square, combination square (which I've sawn short for better access in tight places), carpeted sanding block, beading tool, putty knife, flat scraper, ball-peen hammer, shaved pencil, C-clamps, utility knife, and spring clamps.

Minipumps allow for precise mixing of epoxy used in lapstrake boatbuilding.

Square. Few carpenters, woodworkers, or boatbuilders are without a rafter or framing square. I use my 2-foot square for various jobs, including lofting and marking plywood panels, and to ensure that station molds stand perpendicular to the strongback. The plywood molds, together with the strongback and longitudinal ribbands, form the building jig (see Chapter 4).

Measuring Tools. I have a 30-foot-long carpenter's tape with a 1-inch-wide blade for boat-length measurements. A second 12-foot tape with a 1/2-inch-wide blade is ideal for short jobs. A 2-foot-long wooden folding ruler comes in handy for repetitive measurements in tight places. Fitting the rails is one example. Wood strips, cut to desired lengths, also work well.

I use a 6-inch combination square for marking bevels on planks or laps. A short blade for marking bevels and scarfing joints

works better than a longer one. What's more, it fits neatly into my work apron.

Bevel Gauge. I have a small brass bevel gauge for marking and transferring tight, difficult angles such as those on the breasthooks, rails, and stems. I know of no other tool that's suitable for transferring angles from tight spots. You can see it in action in the photograph on page 67, Chapter 8.

Utility Knife. My Stanley utility, or sheetrock, knife makes precise lines or marks for cutting. Sharp pencils or ballpoint pens also work well, but for greater precision, use a knife. When building a boat, you make thousands of marks and measurements. Precision is crucial.

Clamps. These are among the most important tools for my particular method of building glued lapstrake boats. I use Fuller 2½-inch C-clamps with deep throats and Stanley 83-155 C-clamps when spiling and hanging planks. I have several Jorgensen spring clamps, which I frequently use to hold planks temporarily during dry fitting. Sears Roebuck 2-foot sliding-bar clamps hold the jig securely to the sawhorses and come in handy for other large jobs.

Hammers. As a longtime builder, I have collected various hammers, including several standard-size claw hammers. One that I use often when building ultralight boats is a ball-peen hammer. I use it to drive ¾-inch ring nails, but any other light hammer would suffice.

3
Lofting

To expand a naval architect's drawings into full-scale plans, boatbuilders need a clean, dry place a few feet longer than the boat's hull. Because the boat-shed loft was once considered ideal for this job, those who expanded the drawings became known as loftsmen, and the process resulting in hull lines and cross sections was called lofting.

Unless you have an alternative, such as patterns for hull cross sections,* accurate lofting is essential to boatbuilding. Through lofting, you ensure that the boat you build will have fair lines. Lofting also permits you to detect and correct inaccuracies in architects' drawings before building begins. Limitations of scale in plan drawings mean that measurements are always slightly inaccurate, and these must be compensated for and corrected full scale in the lofting.

After lofting, you will have a good feel for the length and breadth—the actual dimensions—of your boat. Once your plans are drawn to full scale, you could walk on your drawing, almost as though you were stepping aboard for a trial run. (Loftsmen disapprove of this practice.) By lofting full-scale plans, you create a clear, precise image of your boat. In a sense, you see it before building begins.

At times, lofting seems puzzling. Some boatbuilding instructors avoid the subject altogether; others discuss it at length. At least

one 2-hour videotape and several books are available on the subject. But it's not that complicated. Lofting simply means laying out a grid as long and as wide as your boat and then plotting the hull's curves on it. Plotting points come from a table of offsets on an architect's plan.

If you keep this in mind—laying out a grid as long and as wide as your boat, then plotting the hull's curves on it—confusion lessens. Approach the job with a positive "can-do" attitude and you'll succeed. Many people send away for boat plans but balk when confronted by lofting. Once you master lofting, the chances you'll build a fair boat are excellent.

If you have never lofted before, you might try a simple flat- or V-bottomed skiff for your first project. These are less complicated than round-bottomed boats, since their shapes are adequately described by only a few horizontal lines on each side of the hull—the sheer, chine, and bottom for a V-bottomed boat, and only the sheer and bottom lines for a flat-bottomed boat. As an illustration, I'll describe how I loft a simple flat-bottomed skiff. We'll assume that this hypothetical skiff was drawn by its designer to the "inside of plank," as are the skiff designs in Appendix B. This means that the outlines of the boat as you receive them in a plans package from the designer — the profile, or side view; the half-breadth, or plan view; and the body plan, or cross sections — are drawn to the inner surfaces of the planks, transom, and bottom panel. The loft-

---

*To order such patterns for a variety of ultralight designs, see Appendix C, page 127.

ing process is thereby simplified because you do not need to subtract plank and bottom panel thicknesses from the station molds you construct to represent the boat's cross-sectional shape at the various stations. It is only necessary to reduce the mold widths by the thickness of the ribbands on each side of the hull. Many boat plans are drawn to the "outside of plank," which means that plank thickness as well as ribband thickness must be compensated for during lofting. These adjustments are not troublesome unless overlooked, and will be pointed out where applicable as we proceed.

Tools and Materials

We'll start with a description of tools and materials needed for lofting.

Plywood. For lofting, 4- by 8-foot sheets of plywood provide the best working surface. Whatever wood surface you choose, it must be flat and clean, and you must be able to drive small finish nails into it. If possible, buy PTS (patched and touch-sanded) plywood, $5/8$ inch thick. Lay enough sheets to create a working surface about 4 feet longer than your boat. For most canoes and small skiffs, 4-foot-wide plywood sheets allow enough space for both profile and half-breadth views.

Before you begin drawing, whitewash the plywood with thinned latex paint (50 percent water). Lines are easier to see on whitewashed plywood than on a rough, unpainted surface. Always draw with sharp pencils.

You'll use the plywood surface for lofting two full-scale views: a profile view, showing the hull from the side, and immediately above or below it, a half-breadth (or plan) view, showing half of the hull from the top.

Also, you can use this same plywood to make station molds, the cross-sectional pieces of a building jig. But there is a disadvantage in using the plywood for both lofting and station molds. The molds must be cut out of the plywood, and in doing this, you destroy your full-scale plans before building the boat. This poses a problem if you want to return to the full-scale plans to recheck the accuracy of your lofting. Ideally, you'll have one set of ply-

Lofting is done on whitewashed plywood sheets, butted together. In this photo, the author is marking heights for a station mold.

wood sheets for lofting and another for the station molds. How much extra plywood do you need for the station molds? In general, two to four 4- by 8-foot sheets are adequate for boats 10 to 16 feet long.

Steel Tapes. For extended measurements, you need a tape measure at least as long as your hull. I stick with a single tape measure for the entire lofting project. Different tapes have minute discrepancies that can lead to small but significant lofting errors.

Squares. When establishing the grid for lofting, and at various other times, you will need a 2- or 4-foot square. You can make a 4-foot square by cutting a triangle out of a corner of a sheet of plywood. (Make sure the edges are in fact square.) With the proper tool, you can ensure that lines intended to be perpendicular are square to the baseline.

Hammer and Finish Nails. When lofting or creating a line such as the stem, you must plot various points. Then, using a small claw hammer, you'll drive 1-inch finish nails into the plywood to mark those points. About ½ pound of finish nails is enough to loft a canoe or small skiff.

Batten. To check and draw curves, use a ⅝-inch-square, straight-grain batten, 2 feet longer than the length of your intended boat. The stiffer, the better—you will be more likely to achieve a fair curve. Clear white pine or spruce are strong, yet flexible enough to bend easily into curves.

Awl and Pencils. To be as accurate as possible, I mark the starting point of a line with a sharp awl. To mark the lines, I use sharp pencils, and I keep them sharp or have several on hand. Pens are good for drawing heavy lines.

Chalkline. I mark long straight lines such as the baseline of the lofting grid with snapped chalklines. Also, the machine-cut edge of a piece of plywood makes a good straightedge for long lines. I have an 8-foot aluminum straightedge, but don't buy one unless you anticipate using it for other projects. It's expensive and too short for most boats.

A basic lofting grid has a baseline, centerline, and perpendicular station lines spaced on centers, according to your plan.

Laying Out the Grid

To begin the process of lofting, you must first lay out a grid longer and wider than your boat. The grid should be big enough to accommodate two full-scale views: the profile view and, immediately above or below it, the half-breadth view. Begin with the baseline.

Baseline. After whitewashing your plywood sheets, lay them flat. Fasten them together where they butt. To begin the grid, establish a long baseline, parallel to and 1 inch from the bottom edge of the plywood. Give yourself this margin because you might need to drive a finish nail into the baseline. Mark the baseline with a snapped chalkline or a straightedge.

Perpendiculars. Use a large square to draw perpendiculars, also called station lines. Make them absolutely square to the baseline. Accuracy is critical. Space the perpendiculars according to your plan instructions. Typically, small-boat builders draw perpendiculars on centers—12, 20, or 24 inches apart. Begin with the forward perpendicular (FP).

Draw the perpendiculars up the plywood to the top of the sheets. This will give you enough room for both the profile and half-breadth views. Of course, if you're planning a large boat, you'll need additional plywood sheets to create a working surface wide enough to accommodate both views.

Profile View

Having drawn the grid, you're now ready to begin the boat's profile view. This view will show the heights of a flat-bottomed boat's sheer and bottom lines at each perpendicular. Read these heights from the table of offsets, then measure them from the baseline. Start at the stem.

Stem Profile. To plot a stem profile for a small skiff, first use your square to draw short horizontal waterlines from the FP to the next perpendicular, which usually is at station 0. Space these horizontals according to plan specifications. Typically, they're drawn on 3- or 4-inch centers. With an awl, mark points on each horizontal waterline for the curve of the stem. To establish these points, refer to the table of offsets.

Next, mark the stem plotting points with 1-inch number 17 finish nails. Take a stiff batten and bend it along the outside of the stem curve, now indicated by the nails. If all the nails touch the batten and the curve appears fair, draw it. If several nails do not touch the batten, check the accuracy of your measurements. If only one nail misses by about 1/16 inch, don't worry about it. Draw the curve fair.

An alternative to this method of bending a batten around nails and marking on the inside of the batten would be to measure away the thickness of the batten from the plotting points, set your nails, and draw on the outside of the batten. This may be more accurate, because the nails won't interfere with your pencil line.

Sheer and Bottom Lines. Plot and draw the sheerline, again referring to the table of offsets. Mark points on the perpendicular station lines with finish nails. Bend a batten outside the nails, and check the curve for fairness. Follow the same procedures for the bottom line and, if appropriate, the load waterline. The load waterline indicates where the boat rests on the water when loaded to its designed displacement.

Transom. The transom is drawn from an after perpendicular, once again using plotting points from the table of offsets. To help simplify lofting, naval architects typically make the aft perpendicular the aftmost portion of the boat and the forward perpendicular the forwardmost part, although this is not always the case.

Sometimes, dimensions are shown directly on the plans for parts of the boat such as the skeg. At other times, these plan dimensions are omitted. In such cases, you must measure dimensions with an architect's scale ruler directly from the plan drawing, and draw it full scale on the lofted view.

Half-Breadth View

Above or below the profile view, draw a half-breadth view, showing a lengthwise half of the boat as seen from the top. Draw this view on the unused part of the grid. One view will lie precisely above the other. If you extended a perpendicular line through the center of an oarlock in the profile view, it should pass directly through the center of the oarlock in the half-breadth. This is true for all points, such as the transom at the bottom or the stem at the sheer. All points must line up in both profile and half-breadth views.

To plot a half-breadth view work from the forward perpendicular (FP) to the aft perpendicular (AP), marking plotting points (from the table of offsets) on each perpendicular station line. Remember, in the half-breadth view, you're plotting just half the width from a centerline.

Again, check the fairness of the curve by marking the plotting points with finish nails and laying a batten on the outside of the nails. If the batten touches all the nails or is within $1/16$ inch of the nails, and the curve appears fair, go ahead and draw it. If it doesn't, recheck your measuring to see if it corresponds with the table of offsets. If your measuring appears correct, it is possible that a mistake was made in the table of offsets. That's not uncommon. If you find an error in the table of offsets, correct it and draw the curve fair. When lofting a boat that was drawn to the outside of plank, you will have to reduce the half-breadths of the inner stem by the thickness of the planking. The process, though not detailed here, is not difficult, and the necessary information should be provided in the plans and offsets.

Expanding the Transom

To simplify the job of expanding the transom, I depart slightly from traditional methods. Here's how I proceed for a small skiff:

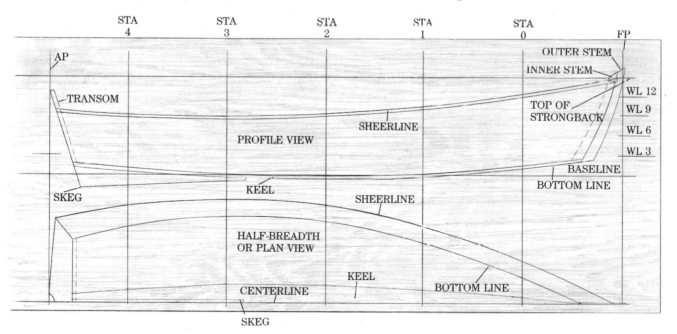

Artist's conception of the profile and half-breadth (or plan) views of a hypothetical skiff. These drawings are not to scale, and do not represent the Flapjack, the building of which is described in this book.

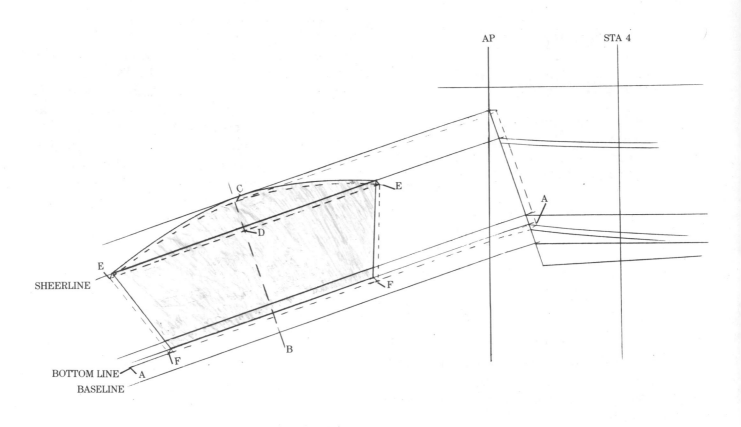

The dashed lines represent the expansion for lines drawn to the inside of plank.

1. Extend a bottom line (A) so that it lies perpendicular to the transom shown in profile view. Then draw a vertical centerline for the expanded transom (B).

2. Mark the centerline with a nail at the maximum height of the transom (C). To determine this height, refer to the profile view. Measure from the bottom of the transom to the maximum height of the transom, then transfer this distance to the centerline.

3. Measure the distance from the bottom to the sheer on the profile view, and mark this distance on the centerline (D). The sheerline runs parallel to the bottom line in a sectional view and should intersect the sheer at the transom in profile view.

4. Refer to the half-breadth view and measure the half-width of the transom at the sheerline. Now, on your drawing of the ex-

panded transom, measure this distance (E) to the right below the sheerline, and mark the point with a nail.

5. Measure the same distance (E) to the left below the sheerline, and mark this point with a nail. You now can scribe a single line indicating the full width of the transom at the sheer.

6. Repeat steps 4 and 5 to establish the full width of the bottom (FF).

7. Connect points E and F to create the two sides of the expanded transom.

8. Now, to get the proper transom crown, refer to the body plan. Depending on the boat you're building, you may need to plot additional points between the maximum height of the transom and the sheer.

9. Bend a batten outside the nails (E, C, E), and draw the transom crown.

You now have a completed transom drawing. You'll use the transom you've just drawn on rough plywood as a "false transom" for your building jig. This false transom serves as a mount for the actual transom.

Before cutting the false transom from the plywood, you must make an actual transom. Transfer the transom shape to your transom stock, then cut it out. (For more details, see Chapter 6.) If the boat is drawn to the outside of the planks, you must reduce the false transom (but not the actual transom) by the thickness of the ribbands and planking combined, on either side of the plywood. For example, if the ribbands are ³/₄ by ³/₄ inch and the planking is ¹/₄ inch, reduce the false transom on either side by 1 inch. You must also reduce the bottom of the false transom by the thickness of the bottom plywood. If the boat is drawn to the inside of planks you need reduce the false transom on each side only by the thickness of the ribbands. Once the sides are reduced, cut the false transom and put it aside. For this cutting job, I use a jigsaw.

Station Molds

Station molds are plywood cross sections of the hull at each station (perpendicular) of your grid. With the station molds outlined, you have the critical information you need to create the molds for a building jig. Once you've drawn and cut them, you're ready to build the jig.

Once again: the profile view provides the boat's heights and the half-breadth view provides the boat's widths. Drawing station molds is a matter of converting those heights and widths into cross-sectional patterns. Do this on clean plywood.

Here's a sequence for drawing station molds on separate sheets of plywood. Refer to the accompanying drawing:

1. Draw a baseline (A), then a perpendicular centerline about a foot higher than the height of your boat (B).

2. Take the heights of the sheer (C) and bottom (D) lines from the profile view, and mark these on the centerline.

3. Take the half-width of the bottom from the half-breadth view, and mark this width by extending a horizontal line out from the centerline in both directions. For example, if half the width of the bottom were 4 inches, you would extend a horizontal line this distance— to the right (E) and to the left (E).

4. Repeat step 3 for the sheerline (F, F).

5. Connect the extremities of the bottom and sheer lines to create an outline of the hull cross section.

6. Mark the height of the top of the strongback (G). (The strongback consists of two parallel pieces of lumber, often 1 x 6s, that support the station molds of the building jig.) The top of the strongback is a few inches above the sheerline.

7. At the top of the strongback, on the plywood, draw a horizontal line (H, H). Draw this line parallel to the baseline and square to the centerline. Extend the sides of the station mold until they intersect with the horizontal strongback line.

Warning: Do not cut the station molds at the sheerline. They must extend to the strongback line, for mounting on the strongback.

Repeat these steps for each station mold. Typically, in a small skiff, there are five to seven stations in a grid. Once you have drawn all your molds, you're almost ready to cut them out.

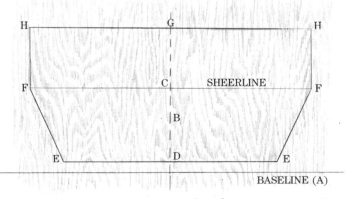

One of the main purposes of lofting is to create station molds, or cross sections, for the boatbuilding jig.

One other step comes first, however. Determine if your boat plans were drawn to the inside or outside of the planks. In the former case you need only reduce the mold widths by the ribband thickness on either side of the molds. In the latter case, you must compensate for the plank thickness as well as the thickness of the ribbands on your building jig. This means you must reduce, or trim, each station mold on each side by the thickness of the ribband and planking. In all cases you must reduce the bottom of the station molds by the thickness of the plywood bottom.

Once you have reduced the station molds, you're ready to cut them out for your building jig. Use care. The station molds must be cut as accurately as possible.

Canoes

If you're building a canoe or round-bottomed boat and your plans are drawn to the outside of the planks, reduce the station molds by the thickness of the planks and ribbands all the way around.

In essence, lofting round-bottomed boat plans involves the same steps as lofting flat-bottomed boats. Canoe and round-bottomed boat plans have more lines to loft, however, and I don't want to minimize the extra work required. Round-bottomed boats require waterlines, buttock lines, and diagonals, and fairing such boats requires that all intersections of these various lines correspond vertically. Once they do, you'll have a fair boat.

While all this may seem complex, the process of lofting is quite logical—much easier than reading about it. I recommend that you loft a flat-bottomed boat before lofting a canoe or any other round-bottomed craft. Try a flat-bottomed skiff, for example, even if you have no intention of building it. The steps will become clear as you work, and incorporating the additional lines and reference points of a round-bottomed craft will prove no problem once the visual logic of the process is evident.

4
Jig Building

Nothing is more important to my boatbuilding method than the building jig. It's the foundation for what follows—making parts such as the stem, transom, keelson, and chines, and then hanging planks. Some people call these jigs forms or molds. I use the term station mold to refer to a jig's plywood cross sections. Regardless of the boat, all my jigs have three basic parts:

Strongback. Just as the building jig is a foundation for boatbuilding, the strongback is the foundation for the jig. I make it from two boards, usually pine or spruce 1 x 6s, fastened at their forward ends and sprung apart amidships with a spreader. The aft ends are fastened directly when a double-ended boat such as a canoe is to be built, or connected with an endpiece for a boat having a transom. I spread the strongback as wide as possible amidships without exceeding the width of the station molds and without stressing the 1 x 6s beyond the breaking point.

Station Molds. These are cross sections of the boat to be built. The primary reason for lofting full-scale plans is to determine the actual proportions of these cross sections. Usually, I make station molds of ⅝-inch plywood. I erect them perpendicular to the strongback, on specified centers. Ribbands then mount on the station molds.

Ribbands. For glued plywood lapstrake construction, these long, narrow battens are an essential part of boatbuilding jigs. I always use clear, straight-grain softwoods, such as cedar, spruce, poplar, or basswood. Even though I wax the ribbands with paraffin, planks are apt to stick to them during gluing. With hardwood battens, the planking might tear when a finished hull was being lifted off the jig.

Ribbands serve six significant purposes: (1) they hold the station molds perpendicular to the strongback; (2) they serve as patterns for tracing plank shapes, thereby making old-fashioned spiling techniques unnecessary; (3) they represent the exact width of the bevels needed to join planks; (4) once a plank is hung, a ribband acts as a guide when you are trimming the plank's rough-cut edges with a laminate trimmer, router, or hand plane; (5) they also guide the modified block plane when you are beveling planks; and (6) each ribband becomes one of two battens that "sandwich" the planks being clamped and glued together.

Skiffs

Typically, my jigs for small flat- or V-bottomed skiffs have one chine and three ribbands per side. These ribbands provide surfaces for the six purposes just described. My skiff jigs have stem and transom profiles, while canoe jigs have neither. A flat-bottomed-skiff jig requires a temporary "backbone" to secure the station molds while you check them for squareness.

Strongback

For most canoe and small-skiff jigs, I prefer 1 x 6 stock for the strongback because it bends without a lot of force. Select or cut the boards about 2 to 3 inches shorter than your boat. (You make up for the difference later.) Also select boards free of loose knots; they might snap when stressed at those points. The 1 x 6s needn't be clear, however; number 2 lumber is satisfactory, but pick naturally straight stock, and remove any crowns in their edges with a plane. (A crowned board will appear humped along one edge when you sight it lengthwise, sagging along the opposite edge.) If *slight* crowns remain, always place the boards so that the upper edge is humped rather than sagging. That way, if the jig settles, you won't have a sagging, or *"hogged,"* hull; if anything, you'll have a little *"rocker."* To repeat: Try to make the 1x6s perfectly straight.

Securing the Ends. Starting with the bow, first secure the ends of the long 1 x 6s with rivets or number 14 bolts and nuts. You need these fasteners (plus gussets added later) be-

cause of the strong outward pressure exerted by the spreader. Nails or wood screws won't hold the ends together.

Square off and secure the aft end of the strongback with a 1 x 6 or 2 x 6 piece. Make this endpiece, or "stern," of the strongback narrower than the width of the transom by a few inches. The exact measurement isn't critical.

Spreader. Once both ends of the strongback are secure, wedge a spreader into position at the widest station mold. The spreader should be about 3 or 4 inches shorter than the maximum beam. Sometimes a hammer helps. If you still have difficulty, cut an inch off one end of the spreader. Place the spreader amidships at the boat's widest station mold, and secure it with 16-penny nails or drywall screws.

Gussets. Now, reinforce the bow and stern corners of the strongback with triangular gussets. Plywood or scrap lumber will do. Once again, secure the gussets with glue and nails.

Finishing the Station Molds

By this point, you have lofted and cut station molds from plywood sheets. Remember,

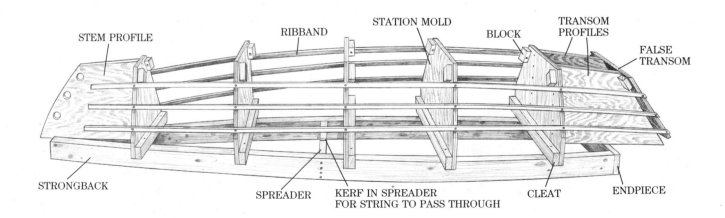

A typical flat-bottomed skiff jig for glued plywood lapstrake construction.

in most cases, you will have to reduce the sides of the molds by an amount equivalent to the thickness of the ribbands and planks, and the bottoms of the molds by an amount equivalent to the skiff's bottom. Naval architects almost always draw plans to the "outside of the planks." So, assuming that's the case for you, reduce the station molds so that your boat will have fair lines and the correct beam. The skiffs in Appendix B were drawn to the inside of the planks, but, as mentioned in Chapter 3, you must still reduce the molds to compensate for the ribbands and bottom panel.

Cleats. Next, rip some 2 x 4s in half, and crosscut this stock into cleats the width of the station molds. Secure the cleats with yellow carpenter's glue (such as Titebond) and drywall screws, flush to the bases of the station molds.

Mounting the Station Molds

To achieve a fair hull, I center the station molds perfectly over the top of the strongback. For this job, a taut, heavy-duty string running down the middle of the strongback is your best guide.

1. Begin by cutting a 1/2-inch-deep kerf, or notch, in the strongback's spreader. The kerf allows you to run the string beneath the station molds without touching them.

2. Next, move to the bow of the strongback, and force the string about 1/4 inch down into the crack formed at the joint of the two 1 x 6s. At the opposite end, force the string into a 1/2-inch cut at the center of the endpiece. Pull the string taut and secure it.

3. After referring to your lofting, measure with a tape and mark the string with a ballpoint pen at each and every station. Begin at the extreme forward end of the strongback and work aft, as though you were marking centers for a stud wall.

4. Hold the tongue of the 2-foot square parallel to but not touching the string, and at each station, mark centers on both 1 x 6s where the edge of the square crosses the strongback.

5. Then, once again working from bow to stern, stand each station mold upright and make sure it is square to the centerline string. Also, make sure the center of each station mold is exactly over the string.

Forward of maximum beam, place all molds flush with and aft of their stations (the pencil marks on the strongback). Aft of maximum beam, do the opposite: place all molds flush with and forward of their stations. If you don't place the molds this way, you won't achieve a fair hull, because you haven't beveled the edges of the molds to fit the curve of the sides. Assume, for example, that the width of a skiff at a station aft of the maximum beam is 2 feet 9 1/2 inches; 5/8 inch farther aft (the thickness of a station mold) the width might be 2 feet 9 1/4 inches. Obviously, then, if you positioned your 2-foot, 9 1/2-inch-wide station mold so that its forward face aligned with the station marks on the strongback, its aft face would be too wide for the inward curving sides of the skiff. Think about that a moment while looking at the drawing on page 24, and you'll see what I mean.

6. Tack or nail a temporary "backbone" (a long piece of 1/2- by 1/2-inch stock) over the top centers of the station molds to secure the molds.

7. Replumb and recheck the station molds for squareness to the centerline and strongback. Now, fasten the molds in place with wood screws driven through the cleats and into the top of the strongback.

Stem and Transom Profiles

Once your station molds stand perpendicular to the strongback, you're ready to attach a stem profile to the bow and transom profiles to the stern of the jig. These plywood pieces provide surfaces to mount and then work on a skiff's actual stem and transom. Profiles are like molds, but they're mounted differently— at right angles to the jig's forwardmost and aftmost station molds.

Stem Profile. How do you get the right shape for the profiles? I take both the stem

Erect station molds square to the strongback. Note the string used to center the station molds.

and transom profiles from the lofting. Simply cut the lofted stem profile out of the plywood with a jigsaw, then mount it square to the station mold.

The stem profile and forward station mold are fastened using two vertical cleats, one on each side of the profile. Before mounting the profile, I bore holes in it as shown in the drawing, leaving about 2 inches of plywood at the forward edge of the profile. Later on, the holes enable me to push mounting rods (1/8-inch welding or brazing rods) through the stem and into the stem profile.

Transom Profile. The transom profile for skiff jigs is more complex than the stem profile. It consists of two identical profiles and a false transom. I mount the latter, a piece of plywood similar in shape to the actual transom, on the trailing edge of the two transom profiles. To make the transom profiles and false transom, follow these steps:

1. Refer to your lofting, and identify the transom profile (in other words, the profile of the stern, aft of the aftmost station mold) on the plywood. Reduce the trailing edge of the profile by an amount equal to the combined thickness of the false transom and the actual transom, if the boat is drawn to the outside of the planks.

2. Then, cut one transom profile from the plywood and use it as a pattern to cut out the second.

3. Refer to your lofting again, and identify the expanded transom. Reduce the width of the false transom by the thickness of the ribbands, as described earlier, and reduce its bottom by the thickness of the skiff bottom. For example, if your ribbands are 3/4 inch thick, take 3/4 inch off each side of the false transom. If your skiff's bottom is to be 1/2 inch thick, take 1/2 inch off there.

4. With the help of cleats, mount the two profiles side by side on the aftmost station mold. Then, add the false transom, and bevel its edges so that the ribbands can land on them. This is necessary because the ribbands are bending in steeply toward the skiff's centerline where they meet the transom, so the after face of the false transom needs to be narrower than its forward face. If you're having trouble visualizing this, don't worry; it will be obvious when you reach this stage in the building.

Lining Off

"Lining off" means adding ribbands and determining the number, shape, and placement of planks. Ribbands, as you will remember, serve as a guide when spiling, hanging, trimming, and beveling the planks. How you place the ribbands determines the planks' width and spacing.

First, though, the ribbands serve another purpose: they keep the station molds perfectly square to the top of the strongback. I always tack the ribbands on temporarily, making sure the station molds are square, and then fasten them permanently. I attach one ribband to one side, proceed to the other side, and attach another, alternating sides so that the station molds won't torque or twist. If all the ribbands were attached to one side before proceeding to the other, the jig could end up twisted.

Ribbands. My ribbands measure ³/₄ x ³/₄ inch, and I make sure the ribbands and chines are of the same thickness. (When you are planking skiffs, the chines have some of the same functions as ribbands.) Cut as many ribbands as you have planks for your skiff, and then cut one other long batten the same thickness as the bottom. That batten becomes a temporary visual guide (representing the bottom thickness) for placing other ribbands.

Before installing the temporary batten and permanent ribbands, add two 2 x 2 blocks, about 4 inches long, to the top of each station mold as shown in the drawing. Later, you will drive screws through these blocks and into the chines. Blocks provide a way to secure the chines with screws from the inside. The screws are removed after planking is completed.

1. Position the temporary batten so that it runs longitudinally on top of the outer edge of the station molds as in the accompanying photograph. As you'll see, the batten simulates the skiff bottom. Starting from the middle and working toward the ends, tack it in place with finish nails.

Aside from representing the skiff bottom, the batten can serve as a guide to make sure the station molds have been drawn and cut accurately. If all the station molds touch the batten their heights are correct. If one or more station molds fail to touch the batten, look for errors in lofting or mold cutting, or for strongback warp.

A temporary batten is tacked into place. This batten represents the thickness of the bottom and serves as a visual aid when lining off (establishing the correct spacing for planks).

To check the topsides for fairness, secure the batten temporarily to the stem and bend it around the outside edge of the station molds. With the batten in this position, again check to see if all the station molds touch it. If one doesn't, check for a lofting error—this time in calculating the width of a station mold. Perform these checks on both sides of the jig.

2. Next, position the sheer ribband and tack it in place temporarily, making sure its outside bottom edge is in fact at the sheerline as marked on the station mold. The inside bottom edge needs to be below the sheerline mark, and playing with it a second or two will tell you how far. Note that the sheerline mark is now somewhat above the corner between the sloping edge and the vertical leg of the mold, because you've reduced the sides of the mold by the thickness of the ribbands and planks (or the ribbands only, for a boat like the Flapjack that was drawn to the inside of the planks). If you align the *inside* bottom edge with the sheerline mark, the outside bottom edge—the one that really counts—will be 1/8 to 1/4 inch too high due to the sloping edge of the mold on which the ribband rests.

Each ribband should extend past the false transom and the stem. Using a 2-foot square, recheck each station mold to make sure it is perpendicular to the strongback.

3. Now, place the second and third ribbands on the station molds. (If you plan to have three planks per side, you will need a total of three ribbands, plus the temporary batten representing the bottom thickness.) Using your own judgment, place these ribbands so that they look properly spaced. Look at other boats to get a feel for proper proportion when lining off planks. (In some cases, the spacing may be specified on your boat plans.)

When checking ribbands for fairness, back off and look carefully. Give yourself plenty of time. I've spent as much as 5 hours lining off a jig. You may even want to turn the jig rightside up. Take a break and look away from your work for a while. If something appears off, you'll notice it. When determining fairness,

there's nothing more accurate than your eye. Most of the time, a batten or ribband "wants to fair itself."

4. Working from the center toward the ends, fasten ribbands permanently to the station molds and false transom with 2-inch number 6 flathead wood screws. Remember to alternate sides in order to reduce the chance that the station molds might twist. If you have difficulty screwing into the edges of the station molds, or at points with severe bends, add cleats. Like the blocks for the chines, these have more surface area to hold screws. Either 1 x 1 or 1½ x 1½ blocks work well.

5. Mark the outlines of each ribband on the stem profile, then trim each ribband about 6 inches short of the stem. The marks will serve as a guide when you are spiling and planking. At the stern, trim the ribbands so they're flush with the false transom, and screw them into its beveled side edges.

One final step: You must wax all but the sheer ribbands to reduce the chance that the hull will adhere to the jig during gluing. Most often, I use paraffin, but in a pinch, I'll pull a candle out of a holder and use that.

Canoes

Jigs for my ultralight canoes are similar to those for skiffs, but they differ in a few significant details. Like the skiffs, the canoe jigs require a strongback, spreader, station molds, and ribbands. Unlike skiffs, they have no stem or transom profiles. My canoe jigs do have a permanent backbone, a center batten running along the top of the jig.

Strongback

For canoe jigs, I fasten together two 1 x 6s at both ends and push them apart with a spreader to create a double-ended strongback. The strongback should be about 6 inches shorter and 6 inches narrower than the planned dimensions of the canoe. The 1 x 6s are number 2 lumber, free of large, loose

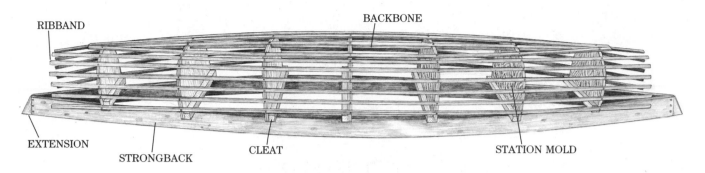

RIBBAND   BACKBONE   EXTENSION   STRONGBACK   CLEAT   STATION MOLD

A canoe jig for glued plywood lapstrake construction. (The spreader is not shown because it is obstructed by the center station mold.)

knots. Place them with the crowns, if present, facing up.

Secure the ends of the 1 x 6s with rivets or number 14 bolts. Then, wedge a 1 x 6 or 2 x 6 spreader, a few inches narrower than the widest station mold, amidships between the long 1 x 6s. Fasten the spreader with 16-penny nails or drywall screws. Later, small wood extensions will be added to the ends of the strongback (see page 41).

Finishing the Station Molds

Reduce the station molds all around by an amount equivalent to the thickness of the ribbands and planks. Add cleats, securing them with glue and drywall screws. Fasten the station molds to the strongback (see "Mounting Station Molds," steps 1 through 5, page 25).

Adding the Backbone

Once you've mounted the station molds, add a backbone to the exact top center of the jig as in the accompanying drawing. Cut notches in the station molds deep enough to accommodate the backbone and part of the keelson (enough to give the keelson's upper surface the same clearance above the molds as the ribbands). Replumb and recheck the station molds for squareness to the centerline and strongback. The backbone (a batten of $3/4$- by $1^1/2$-inch stock) holds the station molds perpendicular to the strongback. Later, it will serve another purpose: the canoe's keelson mounts on top of it.

Lining Off

Add ribbands, essentially following the steps described in "Lining Off" (pages 26–28). Begin with your sheer ribband, and space the remaining ribbands evenly between it and the backbone. Most of my canoe jigs have six or seven ribbands per side. At both the bow and stern ends, cut the ends of the ribbands about 6 inches short of the full length of the canoe. Wax all but the sheer ribbands with paraffin or candle wax.

5

Scarfing

All the boats I build measure at least $9^{1}/_{2}$ feet, and that makes them at least $1^{1}/_{2}$ feet longer than my planking material, standard 4- by 8-foot marine mahogany plywood sheets. I cut the 4- by 8-foot sheets in half to make 2- by 8-foot panels, then I scarf these together end-to-end, creating panels a few inches longer than the length of the boat at the gunwale. These panels are the stock from which I cut finished planks. A scarf joint comprises two beveled, overlapped ends that are glued together. Because the glue has great strength, the scarf joints are durable and watertight. For aesthetic reasons, I position the planks on the hull so that the joints don't line up one above another.

In most cases, three or four sheets of 4- by 8-foot plywood suffice to build boats $9^{1}/_{2}$ to 16 feet long. From your plans, you can calculate the amount of plywood you'll need. Make the scarfed panels at least 4 to 6 inches longer than your boat at the sheerline. Then, when you cut your scarf joints, you'll have a margin for error. Hudson Marine Plywood Company will scarf together panels to any length, if you prefer to go that route (see Appendix C, page 127).

Cutting Panels. Rip the 4- by 8-foot sheets to create panels measuring 2 by 8 feet. For this job, I use a jigsaw or a Skilsaw. The cut needn't be perfectly accurate because the planks will be cut further from these panels. To save time, stack the 4- by 8-foot sheets, and cut two at a time.

Preparing for Scarfing. Place a piece of scrap plywood about 25 inches long on your workbench, one long edge of the scrap being flush with the end of the bench. Now place a 2- by 8-foot plywood panel on the bench and position one end directly over the scrap, flush with the edge of the bench, so that the end is fully supported yet free for working. The scrap provides a smoother bearing surface than the typical workbench, and a smooth, even bearing is critical when cutting a scarf. Clamp the two pieces to the end of the workbench. When cutting scarfs, always orient the factory edge of the panel you're cutting toward the same side—either front or back—of the workbench. This ensures that when you glue the panels together, the finished, factory edge of both will fall on the same side. I protect the panel from dents by placing small wood pads between my C-clamps and the mahogany surface.

With the panel secure, you're ready to mark it for scarfing. To do this, you must first determine the scarf width, which should be approximately six times the thickness of the plywood. If your plywood is 4 millimeters thick, make the scarf 1 inch wide; if your plywood is 8 millimeters thick, make the scarf 2 inches wide.

Mark a scribe line with a sheetrock knife, using a combination square set at the scarf width as a guide. Make a mark not more than $^{1}/_{64}$ inch deep. All you need to do is scratch the surface.

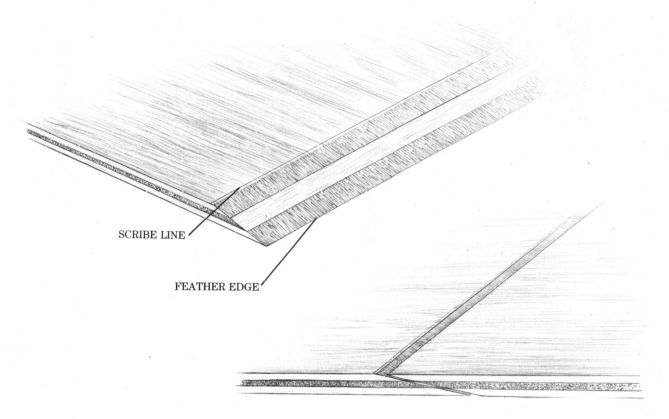

SCRIBE LINE

FEATHER EDGE

To make plywood panels long enough for planks, it is necessary to scarf together two or more lengths. To familiarize yourself with scarfing, practice on scrap plywood. When gluing, leave the feather edge of one piece about ¹/₈ inch shy of the scribe line on the other. This ensures that the plies of the two pieces line up when viewed in section.

Cutting the Scarf. A low angle block plane is the tool to use for scarfing plywood. Because you will be cutting across the grain, keep the plane iron razor-sharp at all times (see Appendix A). Shallow adjustment of the plane iron is critical so that it shaves the smallest possible amount of wood.

Slowly and carefully bevel across the end of the panel, working the scarf down at the edge of the plywood first. Then, plane back toward your scribe line, creating an increasingly wide scarf.

Aim to make the cut perfectly flat—from the line down to your feather edge. Take your time. Push your plane in continuous straight strokes across the end of the panel. Never shave off the scribe line. If you do you change the width of the scarf.

As you continue, the plies plane back and begin to look like bands. Try to plane so that the bands remain perfectly straight. If they're straight, and parallel with the scribe line, you're planing a flat scarf. Also, try to give the bands a uniform width with one exception: the feather-edge band may be slightly narrower. Repeat this process until you have cut scarfs on all the panels required for your boat.

Gluing Scarf Joints. To prepare for gluing, place a piece of plywood about 6 inches wide and 30 inches long on your workbench, and cover it with a piece of plastic big enough to underlay the scarf joint. The plastic acts as a release agent so that you don't glue the panels to the workbench.

Place the two panels you intend to join

Before cutting a scarf, mark the length of it with a very shallow scribe. A scribe is more accurate than a pencil line. When planing, always leave the line untouched.

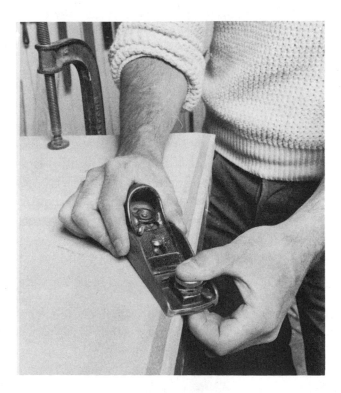

When cutting scarfs, hold the plane at a slight angle to the direction of travel.

end-to-end with the axis of the joint over the plastic, making sure they are flat. To test for flatness, overlap the scarfed pieces and press down at the joint. The two pieces should remain in a neat fit as you press down. Clamp one of the panels, with the scarf cut facing up, to the table.

Next, flip the other panel so that its scarf cut also faces up. Then, with a small, disposable acid brush, available through hardware and plumbing supply stores, apply glue to both scarf cuts. Brush on enough glue so that the surfaces appear wet and shiny, and let it soak for about 5 minutes so that the wood is well saturated. My tendency is to go heavy with the glue. People on the water depend on these joints, so I don't short them. On the other hand, I avoid globs of excess glue that might keep the wood from touching or lead to bothersome sanding jobs.

Now, fit the two scarfed panels together, leaving the feather edge of the top panel about 1/8 inch shy of the scribed knife mark on the bottom panel. If you don't do this, the grains of the plies won't line up neatly, and this lack of alignment will create a bump at the joint.

Clamping the Panels. Check both panels for lengthwise alignment with a long straight-

After applying glue to a scarf joint, clamp the plywood panels to your workbench, then sandwich them between plastic sheets and two boards. Add a weight to the top for good measure.

edge or a string. Once they're aligned, clamp the second panel firmly to your working surface, so it can't slide.

Place a second piece of plastic over the scarf joint. Then place a ³/₄-inch-thick scrap board, about 6 inches wide and 30 inches long, over the plastic and the joint. Clamp the stock so that it holds the scarf joint firmly to the workbench.

With my clamps, I estimate I bring down about 100 pounds of pressure on the joint. But I go one step further. I add a 70-pound metal weight on top of the scrap wood. (In the win-

ter, I store the weight on my woodstove. When I am gluing joints, the warmth from the metal hastens the curing process.)

Allow the glue to dry for about 2 to 3 hours at room temperature. Drying time is shorter in the summer and usually longer in the winter, depending on the temperature in the shop. Often, I do this work at the end of the day so that the glue has plenty of time to dry overnight. Once it has dried, I smooth the scarf joints on both sides with a 4 x 4 vibrator sander.

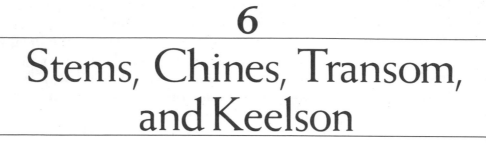

6

Stems, Chines, Transom, and Keelson

By now, you've completed the jig for a flat-bottomed boat or a canoe, but you haven't yet built a single piece of the boat. That's about to change. You are now going to start cutting, shaping, and installing stems, transom, chines, and keelson, which serve as the starting point for planking the hull.

To illustrate the glued plywood lapstrake technique I use, we will be building the Charlotte, an 11½-foot, round-bottomed canoe, and the Flapjack, a 14-foot, flat-bottomed skiff designed by Steve Redmond. Now is the time to make stems, chines, and a transom for a flat-bottomed boat, or stems and keelson for a canoe.

Skiffs

The Flapjack has two chines, a stem, and a transom, the chines (or chine logs) being longitudinal pieces placed where the bottom and sides of the boat intersect. The transom, of course, is the thick transverse planking at the stern. The skiff's stem has two parts, an inner stem and an outer stem, also known as the cutwater.

Stem

To build a stem for this skiff, I first make a pattern for both the inner and outer stem, which comes either directly from the boat

plans or from lofting. The pattern should have a curved line down the middle separating the two stems.

Place the pattern over a piece of 1½-inch-thick mahogany stock (or whatever wood you're using), and trace it. Spring a batten to the curved joint between the stems, and scribe the line. With a band saw or jigsaw, cut both stems out. This leaves you with roughly cut stock. Compare the stem pieces with their original lofted shapes, and clean them up so that the lines match. Put the outer stem aside; it will be installed later, after planking.

Mounting the Inner Stem

Clamp the inner stem directly onto the stem profile of your building jig, and using a ballpoint pen and a combination square, draw a line down the exact center of the stem's forward edge. Bore three evenly spaced ⅛-inch holes directly through the centerline and into the stem profile's holes. Next, drive ⅛-inch brass rods through the stem and into the profile. Countersink them about ⅛-inch so that you won't nick your plane iron when beveling the stem.

Chines

For the Flapjack's chines, I use ¾- by 1½-inch mahogany, cut slightly longer than the length of the bottom and always the same thickness as the ribbands. When bent around the building jig, the chines exert a lot of outward pressure, so I secure them well with screws, clamps, and gussets to fasten them to the stem, station molds, and transom. Here's how:

After removing the temporary batten on the top edge of the building jig, begin work on the first chine. Place the forward end of the chine at the stem, mark a compound angle on it, and cut it at that angle so that it fits neatly behind the stem. After repeating these steps for the second chine and gluing both chines to the stem, secure them there by fastening a plywood gusset with screws driven down into the chines.

Then, working on one side of the jig, secure a chine to the forwardmost station mold by driving a number 12 flathead wood screw from inside the jig, through the 2 x 2 block, and into the chine. Be careful not to go through the chine, but drive the screw deep enough so that it grabs the wood firmly. Working aft, continue attaching the chine to the jig, securing it with screws driven through the 2 x 2 blocks at each station mold. The inside edge of the chine should be flush with the corner of each station mold.

Let the chines run beyond the false transom by at least a few inches, then clamp them at the false transom. If your boat hull bends sharply aft of the last station mold, you can reduce stiffness in the chine by following this procedure: Wrap the chine in an old blanket and pour boiling-hot water over the blanket. Wrap it with plastic and let it sit for about an hour. After this treatment, the chine limbers up. Once the chines are clamped, trim their ends flush with the false transom. They are now ready to be glued to the transom.

Transom

The Flapjack calls for a transom of 3/4-inch stock. To make it, I joint the edges of two pieces of 3/4-inch mahogany, which, when glued together, will create a single panel wider and larger than my intended transom. On occasion I find a single mahogany plank that's

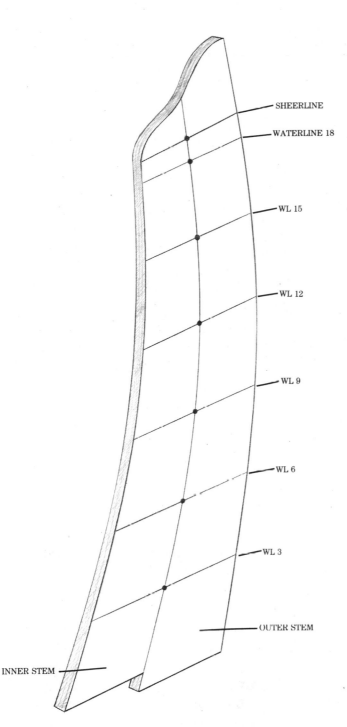

SHEERLINE

WATERLINE 18

WL 15

WL 12

WL 9

WL 6

WL 3

OUTER STEM

INNER STEM

A pattern for the inner and outer stems of a skiff can be cut from the lofting board or traced on paper. Note the sheer and water lines. The outer stem is longer than the inner stem due to the thickness of the bottom and keel.

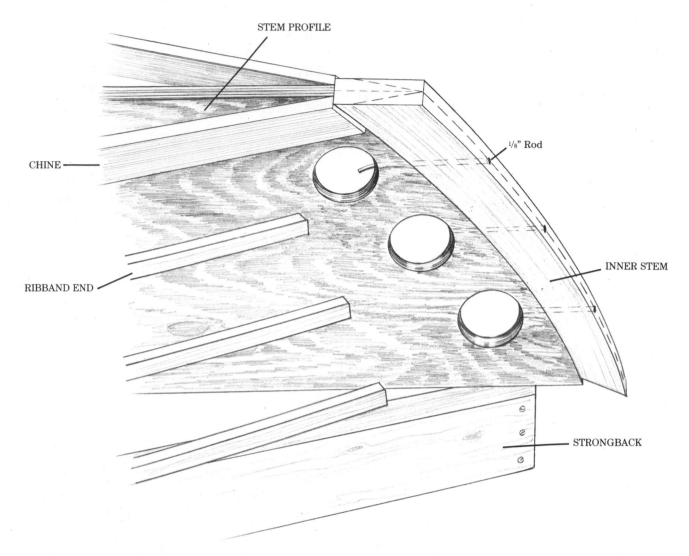

STEM PROFILE

CHINE

RIBBAND END

1/8" Rod

INNER STEM

STRONGBACK

Chines butt to the inner stem, which is mounted on the stem profile with countersunk 1/8-inch rods. Later, when planking, don't forget to pull the rods out.

wide enough for the job, but most often I butt and glue together two pieces of whatever dimension 3/4-inch stock is available. How much wood you need, of course, depends on your boat's transom width. The glue joint should run horizontally across the finished transom. Although I have, on occasion, splined or doweled this joint, it is by no means necessary to do so.

Next, make a transom pattern, obtained from your lofting, and place it over the mahogany. Trace the pattern and cut out the tran-

som. This done, apply glue to the ends of the chines and the corresponding spots on the transom. (Always apply glue to both pieces.) Next, clamp the transom so that it centers on the false transom and contacts the chines.

Shaping the Inner Stem

The object of this step is to plane the rough-cut stem into a symmetrical, almost pointed V, so that the planks will land on it neatly and precisely.

A temporary gusset holds the chines at the stem until the first planks (in position in this photograph) are hung. Note the vertically oriented cleats on either side of the stem profile at Station 0; they run the full height of the station mold.

Tools. As always, work with sharp tools. I begin shaping with a drawknife, followed by a low-angle block plane. To save time, I make deep cuts first, then adjust the plane iron for shallower bites. Next, I make finer cuts with spokeshaves, beginning with the 9-inch and following with a 3-inch modelmaker's shave. Occasionally, I work with a randomly cut rasp. To check the angle I'm cutting, I hold the long rasp over the stem and onto the ribbands as though it were a piece of plank stock.

Beveling the Stem. To cut the exact bevel on the stem, hold a scrap piece of 3-foot-long planking stock flat against the ribbands and stem. This piece takes the place of the actual planks and facilitates planing the exact bevel. Starting at the chine, work down from one ribband to the next until you reach the sheer, and work from the centerline of the stem back toward the bearding line (the place where planking first contacts the stem).

As you plane the sides of the stem (always cutting with the grain), constantly check the

Planing the final bevel on the inner stem of a skiff. Check the bevel periodically by holding a scrap piece of planking stock flat against the ribband and stem.

angle you're cutting. Shave off some wood, then reposition the plank scrap. Look carefully down at the stem from the top, then up at it from below the plank scrap, checking for humps, depressions, or slits of light shining through where the plank and stem meet.

Continue planing as necessary. Reposition the plank. Make further checks. Feel the stem with your thumb and forefinger, making sure the face is flat rather than rounded. When shaping wood, your sense of touch is an important asset.

Beveling the Transom

To bevel the edges of the transom, follow the same method used for the stem. When you align a plank with the ribbands and across a transom edge, it should fit neatly. Bevel from the bottom to the sheer, working with the grain. To avoid a hump or hollow in the bevel line when viewed from astern, use a straight-edge as a guide.

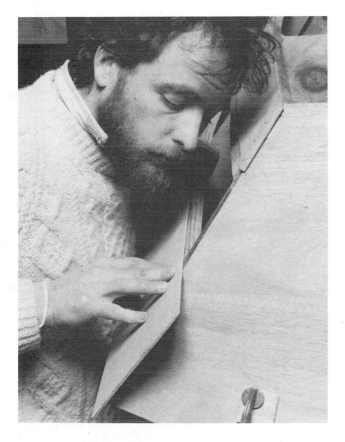

Checking the transom bevel for the sheer plank.

Canoes

My canoes have two identical stems and a keelson. The keelson mounts directly on the backbone of the building jig, and the stems attach to either end of the keelson, creating a continuous, spinelike piece.

The Keelson

I use ³/₄- by 1¹/₂-inch spruce, about 6 inches longer than the length of the canoe. Northern white spruce has a good strength-to-weight ratio, but substitutes such as pine or cedar will also work. Early aircraft designers often preferred spruce because of its lightness, stiffness, and strength.

Having selected your stock, place the keelson on top of the jig's backbone and center it precisely. Secure it with clamps, all mounted on the same side. That way, you can sight down the free edge of the keelson without having your line of vision obstructed by a clamp.

Now, gather together a handful of 1¹/₄-inch number 8 flathead wood screws, go beneath the jig, and drive the screws up through the bottom of the backbone and into the keelson. For a 12-foot canoe, about five or six evenly spaced screws (one between every station mold) will hold the keelson firmly. Once the screws are in, double-check to make sure the keelson lies straight and true on the backbone.

With a combination square and ballpoint pen, draw a heavy line precisely down the keelson's center. This centerline will serve as a guide when you bevel the keelson for planking. (Garboards will butt directly over this line.) Make the centerline deep enough so that you're unlikely to shave it off accidentally when beveling. As with scarfing, always leave your line.

Stem

For canoe stems, I prefer 1¹/₈-inch-thick cedar. Cedar is both lightweight and rot-resistant, and its softness allows it to be shaped quickly. Spruce or pine also works well.

I cut two stem pieces (see the accompanying drawing) from cedar stock, glue them together, and add a facing strip of 4-millimeter-thick mahogany plywood. This piece increases strength and looks good from inside the canoe. To make your stems, follow these steps:

1. Refer to lofting to create a pattern for the stem.

2. Saw out the two pieces of the stem proper. Glue and clamp together the cedar (or whatever wood you're using), aligning the grains as shown along the butt joint.

3. Allow the glue to dry for 3 hours at room temperature. If it feels tacky, it's not yet cured. Once the tackiness is gone the glue is hard enough.

4. Smooth the stem's curved, inner surface with a spokeshave. Use a block plane to square and flatten the surface that attaches to the keelson.

5. Cut a 4-millimeter mahogany-plywood strip about $1/8$ inch wider than the stem's thickness. Bend and glue the strip to the stem and secure it with clamps and pads. As you bend the plywood, inner laminations may crack, but I don't replace the strip unless the outer veneer breaks. If necessary, hold a pot of boiling water beneath the plywood facing strip to limber it up with steam. Once the strip is glued fast, remove the clamps and clean the stem with a plane to a thickness of 1 inch.

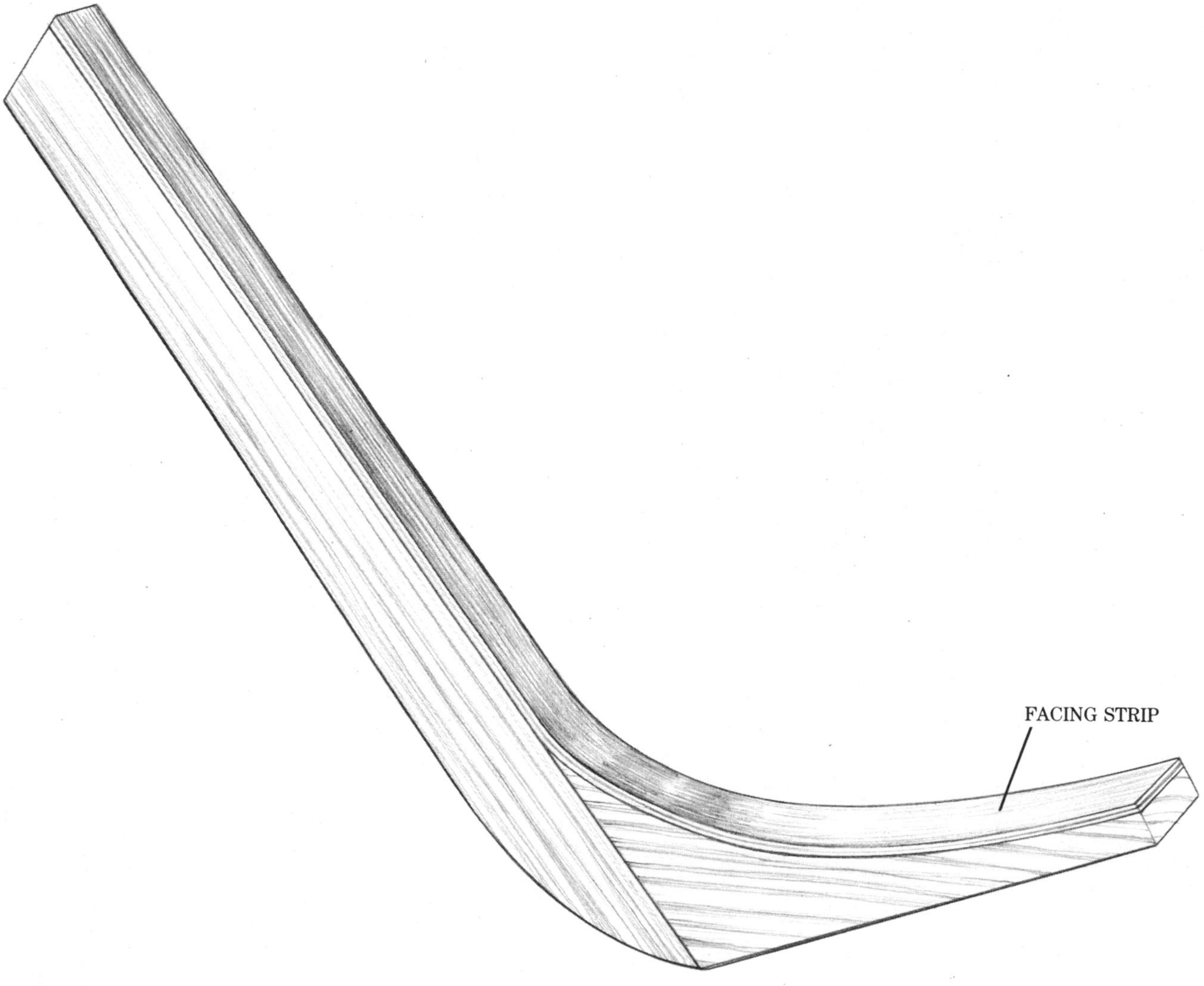

FACING STRIP

To avoid short grain, make canoe stems from two pieces, adding a thin plywood facing strip.

Mounting the Stems

Because you made the strongback shorter than the canoe, you must add an extension, a small piece of wood at each end, for mounting the stems. The first step, though, is to clamp the stems to the keelson temporarily.

Then, by measuring from stem to stem at the sheer, below the strongback, you can determine where to position the stems on the keelson so that your boat has exactly the desired length. Position the stems so that they're equidistant from the first and last station molds. Now that you've determined where to mount the stems, mark their positions on the underside of the keelson.

The small jig extensions will secure the stems temporarily to the strongback at the sheer. Make a wedge-shaped piece of wood that complements the angle of the inside face of the stem. The piece should also have the same side-to-side thickness as the stem. Attach it to the end of the strongback with screws, nails, or glue, and make another for the other end. Clamp the stems to the extensions, using pads to bridge the joint and protect the wood (see the accompanying photograph).

Once the glue has dried, cut off the excess keelson square-edged exactly at the point where it leaves the stem. Remove all clamps except those holding the stems to the jig extensions.

Beveling the Keelson and Stems

You have already drawn a heavy centerline straight down the middle of the keelson. With

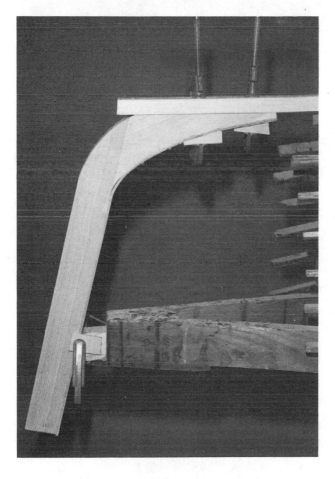

Glue and clamp the canoe stem to the keelson and to the short strongback extension. Note the wedges and clamp pads.

Bevel the canoe stem with a spokeshave or plane. The job will be easier if you brace the stem by leaning down on it.

a combination square and a ballpoint pen, continue that line along the center of the stems. This done, you're ready to bevel both the stems and keelson. The aim is to produce a continuous winding bevel, a surface cut with a variable angle. As you plane, the stems and keelson will look more and more like a single piece.

Begin working on the keelson with a low-angle block plane fitted with the special guide

To check your bevel, place a piece of scrap planking across the stem and ribband and make sure it lies flat. The same procedure is followed when beveling a skiff's inner stem.

(see Chapter 2, page 6), the guide riding on the garboard ribband. I make long passes the length of the keelson, rather than short, choppy strokes. Check the bevel by holding a straightedge from the garboard ribband to the centerline on the keelson.

Keep the plane iron sharp (Appendix A), and work slowly. You'll begin to take off wood all along the keelson, but you'll reach the centerline first amidships, where the angle of the bevel will be less severe. As you get closer to the line, back the plane iron off so that you take less of a bite.

Seen straight on from the front, the forward edge of the keelson will assume the shape of a small, almost perfect triangle. Once it has that shape, continue onto the stems. While shaping a stem, use a 3-foot-long piece of scrap plank stock as a guide (see "Shaping the Inner Stem," page 36). Check and recheck your planing, both by sight and touch.

When correctly beveled, the keelson and stems appear to be a single continuous piece, with smooth transitions where they join. Seen from the side, a stem and keelson form an even, uninterrupted curve.

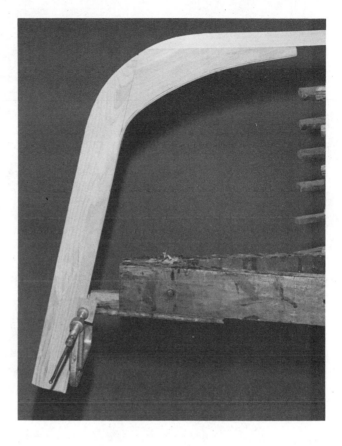

A finished stem attached to the keelson. Note the smooth, curved transition from keelson to stem.

7

Planking

A building jig simplifies the job of planking, because pairs of the jig's ribbands form patterns for tracing plank shapes. Each ribband represents the exact width of the bevel needed to join planks, and the ribbands act as guides for trimming and beveling. Finally, they enable you to glue planks together in place on the jig.

Skiffs

The Flapjack has three 1/4-inch-thick (6-millimeter) planks per side. The planking stock is two 2-foot-wide, mahogany-plywood, scarfed panels, each about 14½ feet long, one panel sufficing for all three planks on a side. After the sides are planked, I bevel the chines and fasten on the ½-inch-thick bottom.

Spiling. Spiling is a term used for transferring the shape of a plank onto planking stock. While there are many ways to spile a plank, I do it by tracing the shapes from the ribbands on the building jig.

Clamp a 2-foot-wide panel to the chine and first ribband, using C-clamps and pads to protect the plywood. Make sure that the panel lies flat against both chine and ribband, and clamp it so as to waste no more wood than necessary. Next, crawl beneath the jig and trace out the plank with a pencil that has been shaved so one side is flat (see photograph, page 12), tracing along the upper edge of the chine and

the lower edge of the ribband. You can't trace the plank all the way because the ribband ends short of the stem. So, after tracing as much as you can of the first plank, return the planking stock to your workbench. Clamp the panel onto the second 2-foot-wide panel, and extend the bow end of your ribband line with a batten. Then cut out both planks at once (I use a jigsaw for this), leaving the ends long for now.

Before gluing on the first plank, spile the second plank.

Grab the bottommost of the two panels from the workbench, and carry it back to the boat to trace the second plank shape. (Alternating the two panels for tracing plank shapes in this way ensures that the scarf joints are staggered rather than aligned one on top of another in the finished boat. Be sure you don't end-for-end a panel on the workbench, however, or you'll cancel the advantage). Insert small plywood spacer pads (of the same thickness as the planking) between the upper edge of the plywood panel and the ribband, to represent the thickness of the first plank. If you omit these pads, the planks won't fit. Once the panel and pads are clamped, trace the plank with a pencil, marking along the upper edge of the upper ribband and the lower edge of the lower ribband. Make sure the panel lies flat against the lower ribband.

Once again, remove the panel, take it to your workbench, and extend the forward ends of the ribband lines with a batten. Leaving 1/8

44

inch, saw along the line that was traced over the upper ribband, and plane this curve fair. Then saw the plank out of the panel by cutting along the line traced under the lower ribband, leaving 3/16 inch proud of the line. This edge gets planed after the plank is hung on the jig.

Now, you can glue and install the first planks, remembering to apply glue to both the planks and the chines. Hold the planks to the chines with C-clamps and a batten running the full length of the chine on the outside of the plank. Nail the planks at the stem and transom with 3/4-inch number 14 ring nails. Trim the protruding plank ends to within 1/8 inch of the stem and transom. Finally, trim the lower edges of the first planks flush to the ribbands with a block plane, laminate trimmer, or router with a flush-trimming bit.

Beveling. Before adding the second plank, you must bevel the first so that both planks fit together. The width of the bevel is the same as the width of the ribband. With a combination square, mark that width on the outside of the first plank, up from its lower edge.

Bevel the plank with a low-angle block plane fitted with a wood guide. On a flat-sided skiff, the bevel is so shallow that you barely plane through one plywood veneer. But cut the bevel just the same, and don't forget to leave your line.

Gains. On lapstrake boats, the hood ends of the planks are flush with one another rather than overlapping at the stem and transom. To make them so, bevels or tapered rabbets must be cut at the ends. These fits are called gains, the length of a gain being determined by the thickness of the planking and the shape of the bow (and transom). For the Flapjack, I make a gain about 5 inches long.

Begin by making a shallow, 5-inch, horizontal cut with a fine-toothed backsaw on the bevel line where it crosses the stem. This is a tapered cut: Forward, you cut through the full thickness of the planking, but the cut gets shallower aft, disappearing at 5 inches. With a sharp chisel, remove the wood beneath the

When beveling a plank, always make sure your wood guide touches the neighboring ribband.

backsaw cut so as to create a tapered edge. A correctly cut gain leaves wood on about half the stem. On the forward half of the stem, remove all the planking. Do the same at the transom.

Dry-fit your second plank, and see if it fits in the gains. If you have a good fit, the next step (after spiling the third plank) will be to glue the second plank to the first, and clamp it between vertical, 6-inch batten blocks, or "sticks," that sandwich the plank, spanning both ribbands on the inside of the jig and the width of the plank on the outside. (I use batten blocks because my clamps are not deep-throated enough to reach the upper ribband.)

Spile the third planks (or sheerstrakes), following the steps just described. *Remember to spile a sheer plank before gluing and installing the middle plank.* Otherwise you won't be able to trace its shape for spiling.

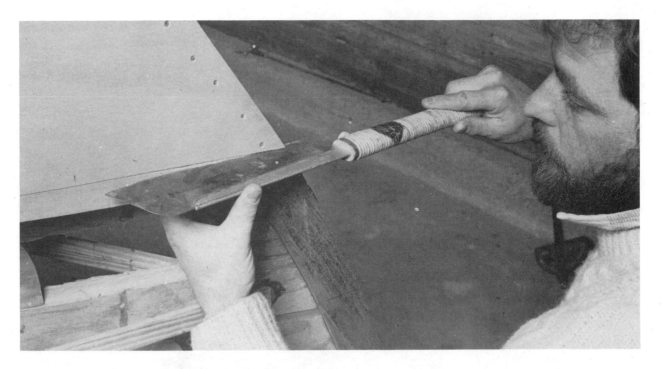

The first step in fashioning a gain on a plank's hood end is to cut along the bevel line accurately with a backsaw. Cut through the entire plank thickness at the end, tapering the cut to no depth 5 inches back from the end. Avoid cutting too deep.

Face the chisel's bevel toward the gain to avoid gouging. Note that each plank is held to the inner stem with five nails.

When you cut the sheerstrake from the plywood panel, saw it out about 1/2 inch proud along the sheerline. That extra inch allows room for cutting errors and makes installation of the rails easier.

Bottom

Planing the Chines. Because of the flare in the hull, you must plane the chines and first planks to a flat surface for the bottom. Notice that the inside edges of the chines are flush to the tops of the station molds. Plane the chines flat to these inside edges with a joiner plane.

Start at the bow and work toward the stern, checking your progress by holding a 2-foot square and a long straightedge across the chines. I find it's easier to get a feel for how my work's progressing if I start from the bow, where the hull is narrower. I plane from the inside to the outside of the chine, making frequent checks for flatness.

I like to bevel the transom while doing the last few inches of the chines. As a guide, I

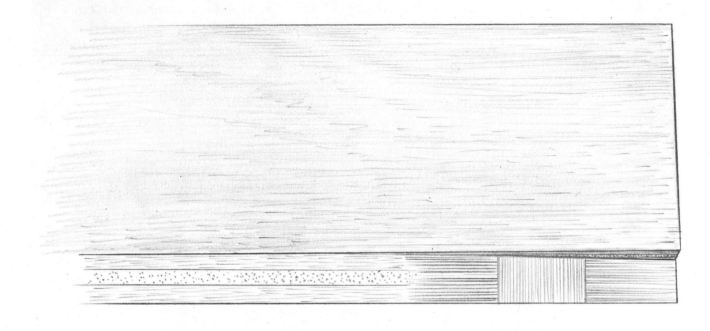

The appearance of the plywood grain in a completed gain.

draw a straight horizontal line across the outside of the transom.

The Bottom. For a Flapjack skiff bottom, I use two 4- by 8-foot, ½-inch mahogany plywood panels, scarfed together to create a single 4-foot-wide panel of the needed length. To save time, the sheets may be trimmed and scarfed right on the skiff bottom. This method is easier and quicker than scarfing and gluing the sheets on a workbench and then attaching a single plywood bottom piece.

To start, draw lengthwise lines down the center of both sides of the plywood. These guide you as you center the plywood over the centerlines on your station molds. Later, the lines serve as references for installing the keel, skeg, centerboard trunk, and mast step.

Flop the first sheet onto the bottom, and match the line on the plywood with the centerlines on the station molds. Place the sheet's factory edge at the transom. Because of the rocker, weight the plywood to bend it down and hold it in position. With a pencil, outline the bottom on the underside of the plywood.

Plane the chines. Use a 2-foot square and a long straightedge to make sure they're level and flat to accommodate the skiff bottom.

Next, mark the width of the scarf you need on this sheet. (I make scarfs 3 to 4 inches wide for ½-inch plywood.) Flop the next plywood sheet onto the bottom so that its factory edge falls on the after edge of the scarf you just outlined.

Trace or outline the remainder of the bottom, the part to be cut from the second ply-wood sheet. Once you have traced the entire bottom onto both sheets of plywood, cut it out with a jigsaw, about ¼ inch proud.

At your workbench, cut scarfs on the ply-wood sheets. (For details on scarf joints, see Chapter 5.) Then follow these steps:

1. Dry-fit and attach the first sheet to make sure it covers the bottom. I use number

When marking the skiff bottom, make sure the centerline on the panel aligns with the centerlines on the station molds.

8 stainless steel wood screws, slightly countersunk and spaced on 5-inch centers. The chines and transom are angled, so drive your screws at an angle, too.

2. Dry-fit the second sheet, then remove it.

3. Remove, glue, and resecure the first sheet with screws, having applied glue to the plywood, chines, transom, and bottommost planks.

4. Glue and again drive screws through the second sheet into the chine. For a fair scarf joint, lay an 8-inch-wide piece of scrap wood over a piece of plastic across the bottom. To make the joint tight, drive screws from the inside of the hull up into this temporary piece.

After the glue has dried, plane the edges of the plywood bottom so they are flush with the bottommost plank and have the same flare as the topsides.

If your plan calls for fiberglassing the bottom, your next job is to fill the screw holes, round the bottom corners at the chines, and then sheathe the bottom with fiberglass and epoxy. Cloth protects the bottom when beaching.

Canoes

Planking a canoe, though similar to skiff planking, requires a few slightly different steps. If you've read the skiff section, some of the following may seem repetitious, but it is essential that all canoe-planking steps be fully described.

Spiling the Garboards

Place two 2-foot-wide, scarfed 4-millimeter plywood panels, one precisely above the other, on your workbench or sawhorses. Align the plywood so that the factory edges of both panels face toward you. Measure the length of each panel, then, using a 2-foot square, draw a line from side to side across each face of each panel, dividing the panel into two equal seg-

ments. Turning to the keelson on the building jig, mark it directly over the center of the centermost station mold. You can now orient the panels to the exact center of the building jig.

Pick up one of the panels and walk to the far side of your jig. (When spiling, or taking plank shapes from your jig, always work on the same side. This ensures that your scarf joints will be staggered.) Flop the panel on the jig so that the factory edge fits precisely on the centerline drawn down the middle of the keelson, and the panel's side-to-side centerline is aligned over the center station mold. Make sure the panel rests flat on the keelson and flat on the first (garboard) ribband. Once it is aligned on the keelson, secure the panel with C-clamps, one next to each station mold. To avoid denting the plywood, insert clamp pads.

When fitting a garboard plank on a canoe jig, the plywood's factory edge lines up with the centerline drawn down the keelson.

Marking. Take a sharp pencil and shave a few inches off one side, making it as flat as possible (see photograph, page 12). To be precise, you must remove the thickness of the pencil wood before outlining your planks. Squat beneath your building jig, look up, and locate the garboard ribband, which runs adjacent to the keelson.

Working from the center to the ends, draw the garboard plank, using the lower edge of the ribband as your guide. As you reach the ends of the jig, you may notice a few places where the panel lifts up off the ribband. While you mark with one hand, reach around and push the panel down onto the ribband. Panels must always remain flat on the lower ribbands for accurate marking.

With the garboard drawn, loosen the clamps, return to your workbench, and lay the marked panel on top of the second panel. Remember to face the factory edges of both panels toward you. Use the centerlines to align the panels, then clamp them together.

Because the ribbands stop short of the stem, the line for the garboard will be incomplete. To extend it, clamp a batten, about 5 feet long, on the plywood, and continue drawing the curve of the garboard. Check the curve for fairness. Complete the line at both ends, and fill in the short blank segments caused by interference from station molds.

Cutting the Garboards. Now you're ready to cut the garboards from both panels. I use a

Small canoes are light enough to tip up when you are marking planks. Note that when marking for the garboard plank, you trace along the lower edge of the garboard ribband, holding the shaved pencil flat against the ribband. The spreader in the strongback is visible at the lower left. One of the clamps holding the factory edge of the panel to the backbone is visible at the upper right.

jigsaw with a sharp, fine-toothed metal-cutting blade to reduce the chance of tears. To give yourself room to play with, always cut $^{3}/_{16}$ inch proud of the line. A plank cut too narrow is a wasted plank.

Now take one of the garboards and return to the jig for a dry fit. Always do this before gluing a plank. Clamp the garboard temporarily so that the factory edge again fits on the keelson. Trim the excess plank flush with the stems. Clamp the other garboard to the other side, and then trim this plank as well. The temptation will be strong to glue your garboards to the keelson immediately. Don't.

Before you hang a plank, always draw the next one.

Second Planks

Take the garboards off the jig and put them aside, then go back to your workbench and grab the *bottom* panel of the pair. By always grabbing the bottom panel, you can be sure that the scarf joints won't line up one directly above the other. They should line up, but only on every other plank. Never "end-for-end" the panels on the workbench (that is, rotate them 180 degrees).

Marking and Cutting. Place the panel so that its freshly cut-out, curved edge is over the garboard ribband, align the panel's centerline with the center station mold, and hold it temporarily with spring clamps. To avoid waste, let the panel extend only slightly above the garboard ribband—never more than $^{1}/_{4}$ inch—at the center station mold.

Beginning at the center, resecure the panel to the ribband with about five C-clamps. I insert small plywood spacer pads (of the same thickness as the planking) between the upper edge of the plywood panel and the garboard ribband. These pads represent the thickness of the garboard plank, helping to ensure a close fit. (Spacer pads are not required for the garboards.) The panel must also lie flat along the next ribband down on the jig (the second ribband). Now trace along the upper and

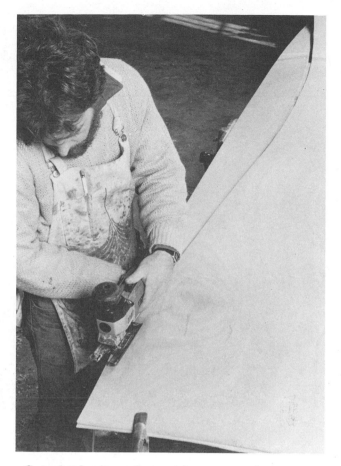

Cut planks in pairs, with one panel on top of the other. Note the spring clamp. While cutting, I support planks with an opened bench vise.

lower (outermost) edges of the garboard and second ribbands, respectively.

Return to your workbench to extend and fill the lines of the plank with a batten. Check the lines for fairness, then clamp the panels, one on top of the other, to your workbench. The plank edge closest to you—the edge that will lap the garboard plank—is cut first. Cut along that edge (cutting both panels simultaneously) with a jigsaw, leaving the line, plus $^{1}/_{8}$ inch.

Fairing the Edges. Next, plane and fair the edges you just cut. Do this final fairing now, before you cut the planks off the panels. If you cut the planks first, you're left with the difficult task of fairing a floppy, long, narrow piece of plywood.

Plane both panels at once, with the two panels clamped together.

You must insert spacer pads, representing the thickness of the adjacent plank, to trace the correct plank shape. Here the second plank, or broadstrake, is shown ready for marking. The keelson is in the foreground.

As you cut the plank edge that will be closest to the keelson when the plank is hung, leave the line plus ⅛ inch.

If there's minor unfairness in the ribband causing unfair lines on the plywood, this is the time to make corrections. I turn the plane around and, always working with the grain, draw it toward me, instead of pushing it. Also, I angle the plane slightly and always hold the plane square to the panels.

Open the plane throat as far as possible to allow shavings to clear easily. As you work toward the line, back off a bit with the iron to take smaller bites. Check repeatedly to see if you're planing a fair curve. Your eye is amazingly accurate: it can pick up $1/64$ inch of unfairness with no problem.

Once you think your edge has a fair curve, make two final continuous passes, starting at the ends and working to the middle, going with the grain. These final sweeping passes give the edge continuity and remove any remaining tiny jagged edges.

Cut out your second planks, leaving $3/16$

With one plywood panel on top of the other, fair the edge you made 1/8 inch proud before you make the second cut to get the planks out of the panels.

inch proud of the line. This edge you will later plane flush to the second ribband on the jig, after the plank has been glued. To keep the plank ends from flopping down as you move the jigsaw forward, support them with a 2-foot square lying flat on your workbench, or a scrap plank slipped beneath the panels.

Gluing the Garboards

Place the two garboards on either side of your jig, resting on the sawhorses. After mixing your glue, brush it on the factory edges of the garboards and on the keelson. (Always apply glue to both surfaces.)

Position the garboards, and, working from the middle toward the ends, drive ³/₄-inch number 14 silicon-bronze ring nails through the garboards and into the keelson. I drive one nail at each station mold, then one between

each station mold. The nails stop at least 6 inches short of the forward edges of the stems. I'm careful not to pound straight down here. If struck too hard, the stems will snap off.

Sheathing the Garboards

I sheathe the garboards with Xynole and epoxy. Sometimes, I substitute a similar cloth called Dynel. I prefer either one over fiberglass because of their abrasion resistance. Also, neither Xynole nor Dynel has the itchy, prickly characteristics of fiberglass. These materials help protect the bottom of your canoe if it should go aground.

First, cut a piece a few inches longer and wider than the garboards and place the cloth over the bottom. Then roll the material back from either the forward or after half of the jig

Nails hold the garboard while the glue dries. They also strengthen this joint.

After applying glue, pinch the garboards tightly to the stem with clamps.

Before sheathing with fiberglass cloth, apply epoxy-microballoon putty to the joint where the garboards meet along the keelson.

When sheathing, always apply glue directly to the wood before covering it with cloth.

and apply glue to the exposed garboards. Strive for an even application (I use a 5-inch putty knife). Once you've done about half the bottom, unroll the cloth over it, stretch it out, and then apply glue over the material. Aim for a smooth, flat, thoroughly wet cloth surface, free of wrinkles, bubbles, or pockets. Then glue the other half. Let the cloth dry, with rough edges extending over the garboards, then trim these edges with a chisel. Later, after completing the planking, add a coating of epoxy-microballoon putty over the garboards.

Trimming the Garboards

For trimming garboards (or any other plank after it's been hung) flush with the ribbands, use a laminate trimmer with a flush-trimming bit, a standard block plane, or a small trimming plane. I begin with a laminate trimmer, a tool that makes the job quick and easy. As before, I start at the center and work toward the ends.

Using the ribbands as your guide, trim as much as possible with the power tool. Where the ribbands end, continue with a plane. *When using a laminate trimmer, be sure to stop where the ribbands end.* If you push too far with this high-speed tool—past a ribband—you could easily ruin a plank.

To complete the trimming with a hand plane, you must mark the last foot or so of the plank with a line that represents the extension of the ribband. To do this, clamp a batten so that its bottom edge is flush with the bottom of the trimmed portion of the plank. Using the batten as a guide, mark the extension. Then plane the plank ends.

When you are doing the final trimming with a plane, repeatedly check your progress.

After spreading the cloth over the garboards, wet it so that it becomes transparent.

After planking is completed, it's a good practice to add a coating of epoxy-microballoon putty over the garboards.

This is another occasion on which you must lower your eyes right down to your work. It's more important to trim the plank to a fair curve than to trim perfectly flush to the ribband. Trust your eye, the ultimate fairing tool.

Beveling

Next, bevel the garboard for the next plank. To mark a bevel for the correct width, I use a combination square set so that its depth equals the width of the ribband. The width of the bevel also equals the width of the lap, or the amount by which the planks overlap. Mark the bevels on the garboards with a ballpoint pen.

Now the low-angle block plane with the special wooden guide comes into use. When beveling with this tool, start from the center and leave your line. Always plane with the grain. Bevel the garboard planks on both sides of the canoe.

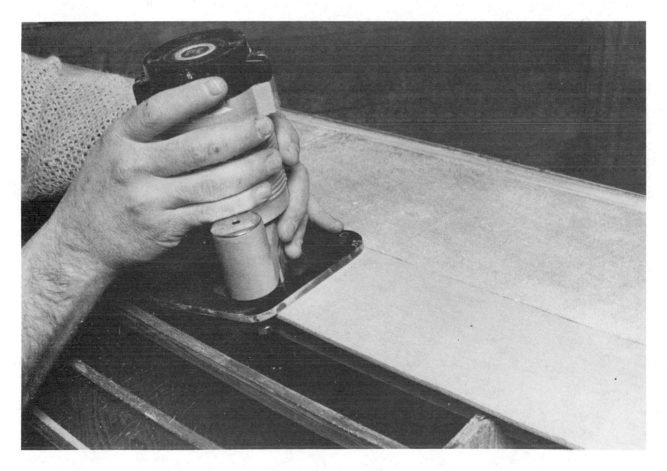

A laminate trimmer (or router) makes quick work of trimming a plank flush to a ribband.

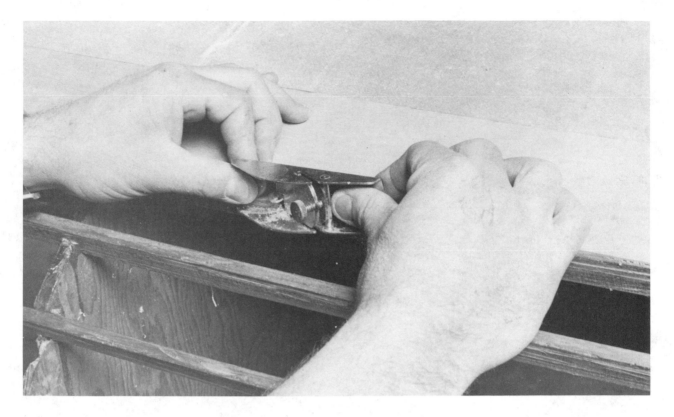

An inexpensive Stanley trimming plane may also be used to trim a 4-millimeter plank flush to a ribband.

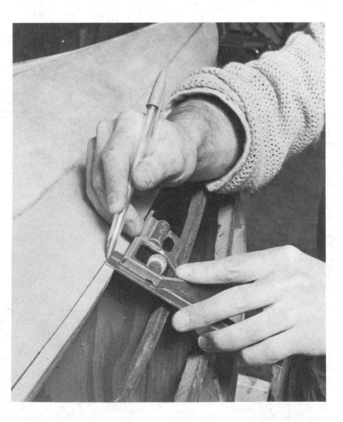

Mark a bevel on the garboard with a ballpoint pen and combination square. Note that the combination square blade has been reduced to 6 inches for easy handling.

Beveling the broadstrake. Note the angle of the plane to the direction of travel.

Cutting the Gains

You must cut gains in the planks to allow room for the hood ends of the next planks to come together in a tight, flush fit. Without gains, planking could not end flush at the stems.

In some traditional lapstrake construction, gains and bevels are cut on a workbench, then fitted on the jig—a process that requires repeated trips back and forth. To save time, I cut the gains and bevel the planks while they're on the jig.

Begin by temporarily securing the second plank in position with just three C-clamps. Next trim the hood ends of this plank 1/4 inch proud of the stems. Use the end of the plank's upper edge to mark the gain on the garboard plank. Also, mark the stem where the lower edge of the plank crosses it. With this reference line on either side of the stem, you can make sure the hood ends of the opposing planks are aligned. If the reference lines don't converge at the front of the stem, you may

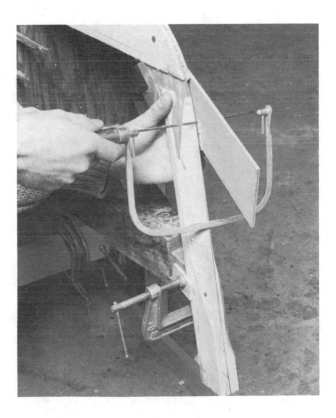

Use a coping saw to trim hood ends preparatory to cutting the gains.

need to shave a bit of wood off one hood end to reduce its width.

Having marked the width of the gain, make a horizontal cut with a Japanese backsaw (or any fine-toothed backsaw) on the bevel line of the garboard hood end for the upper edge of the gain. The cut should penetrate the full thickness of the garboard at the plank end, growing progressively shallower before disap-

pearing approximately 2½ inches from the plank end. With a chisel, cut the rabbet. To avoid gouging deeply, hold the chisel so the beveled edge faces the plank, and try to achieve a gentle taper. Cut so that the planking in the gain covers only the after half of the stem. If the end of the second plank gets in the way, tuck it under the stem.

Once you've cut the gain, release the sec-

You may conveniently tuck a plank end beneath the stem while you cut the gain in the plank above with a backsaw.

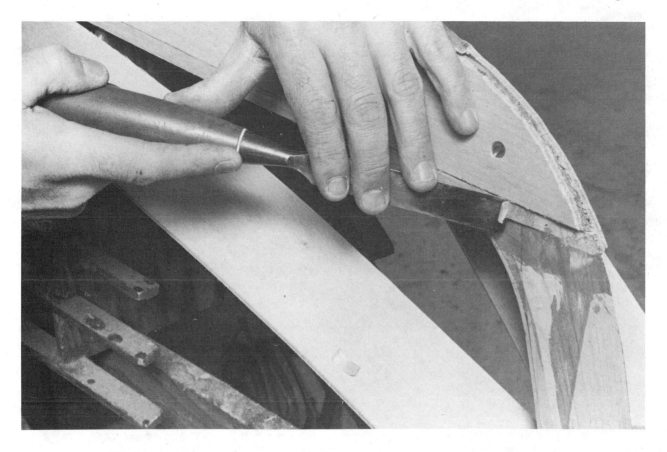

When cutting a gain, use a chisel about ¹/₄ inch wider than the gain.

ond plank, and check the fit. Later, trim the plank flush with the stem so that it won't interfere when you are hanging the plank on the other side.

Repeat the steps for beveling and cutting gains on the other side, and dry-fit the second plank on that side as well. Be sure to mark out the third planks before going on to hang the second planks permanently.

Gluing the Planks

Place the planks on either side of your jig, and apply glue to both planks and the garboard edges. Sandwich a plank in place between the second ribband and a longitudinally oriented batten that's about 1 foot longer than the canoe. Add a clamp about every 6 inches, starting amidships and working toward the ends. Drive one ³/₄-inch number 8 wood screw through the middle of each plank end at the

Apply glue to both surfaces whenever you mate two pieces of wood.

When sandwiching planks together with clamps, start at the middle and work toward the ends.

stems, and countersink it slightly. The screws conveniently hold the plank to the stem while the glue dries. Trim the plank flush to the stems.

Then repeat these steps for the plank on the other side. Although screws hold both planks fast at the centers of their ends, you will also need to hold them with two more C-clamps—one placed at the lower edge, the other at the upper edge. Sometimes, to make the planks fit tightly at the gains, I slip small wedges between the battens and the planks.

The steps outlined above are repeated to get out and fasten the remaining planks. As you progress, the garboard-facing edge of each new plank to be cut out of the panel is approximately represented by the curved edge of the panel left when the previous plank was sawn out. Each time you spile a new plank shape, hold the panel up to the building jig with this freshly cut edge about ¼ inch proud of the uppermost (or inwardmost) of the two ribbands to be spanned by the plank. This method reduces plywood wastage to an absolute minimum, and you can get all the planks for a canoe from three or four scarfed 2-foot-wide panels.

Finally, as for the skiff, leave the sheer-plank edge untrimmed, standing about ½ inch proud of the sheer ribband.

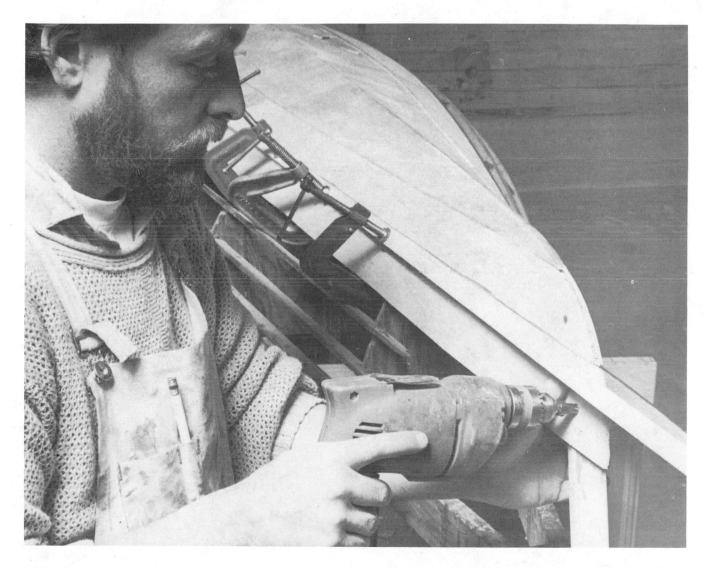

After a plank has been clamped nearly to the stem, drill and slightly countersink a screw through the hood end and into the stem. A gentle touch prevents countersinking too deeply.

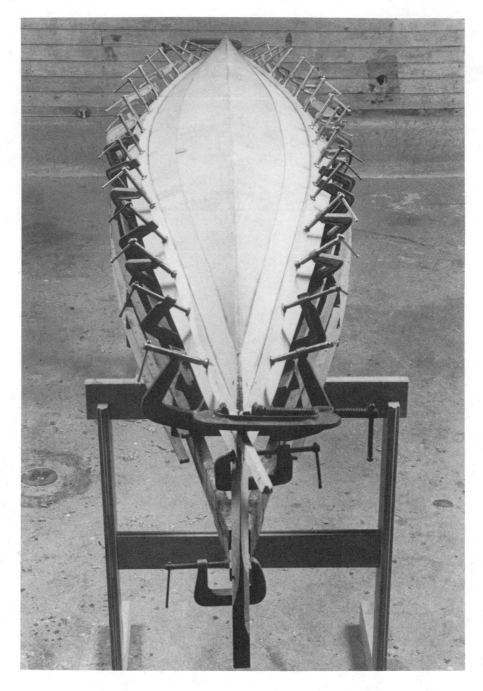

A typical final glue-up and clamping.

8

Joinerwork

After hanging the planks, your canoe or skiff looks like a boat. Even though it seems as though you're almost done, however, you're only about one-quarter of the way to completion. Much work remains, but it involves challenging, enjoyable jobs such as shaping breasthooks and installing rails. Also, at each step of the way, your boat becomes better defined, emerging from a bare hull to a finished craft.

Now, you must select woods for the remaining joinerwork. If you want durable rails, for example, you may choose mahogany. For less weight, spruce is a good choice. Follow your plan carefully. Variations in materials and scantlings can seriously affect a boat's strength and performance. To begin, I'll discuss building techniques applicable to both canoes and skiffs, then continue with specific information for skiffs and canoes, in that order.

Canoes and Skiffs

Rails (Outwales and Inwales)

On the canoe and skiff rails, I use stock of various dimensions, from $5/8$ inch square to $3/4$ by $1^{1}/4$ inches. Follow your design specifications. There are two inwales and two out wales, which, together, add a great deal of strength to the hull. Rough-cut four rails about 6 inches longer than the boat to adjust for the

hull's curve. Also cut a fifth rail, to be chopped up into spacer blocks and placed between the inwales and sheer planks. I plane this rail to a thickness of about $3/8$ inch for canoes or $1/2$ inch for the skiffs.

Remembering that the sheerplank edges were left untrimmed, draw a line on the outside of each sheerplank to represent the sheerline. The top of the rail (facing down when the boat is upside down) aligns with the sheerline. To draw these lines, make tick marks on the outside of the planks at the sheer, using the bottom edge (that is, closest to the floor in the upside-down position) of the sheer ribbands as a reference. Make a mark at each station mold, then connect the marks by drawing with a pencil along a batten clamped to the sheerplank.

Check the line for fairness. A rail bent along this line bends fairer than the ribband behind it, because the rail is longer than the ribband. Therefore, the line and rail—not the ribband—ultimately determine the sheer. After drawing your sheerlines, remove the batten and clamps.

Canoe Stem Bands

Before attaching the outwales to a canoe, put a stem band on the very outside edge of either stem. (On a skiff, you may need to add an outer stem, or cutwater, if required by the particular design. See "Skiff Outer Stem" below.) This protects the stem and bottom

65

from damage if the canoe runs aground. I make stem bands from half-oval brass strips, 3/8 inch wide and 24 inches long. The bands come in 12-foot sections and are available at good marine hardware stores.

For the band to fit neatly, you must plane the forward edge of the canoe stem to a width of 3/8 inch. Measure from the sheerline upward and onto the keelson a distance slightly longer than the length of the band. For me, that would be 24 1/8 inches. Make a mark and plane to that point.

Next, using a 3/32-inch drill bit, make holes in the band 4 to 5 inches apart, then countersink the holes slightly so that they will accept nailheads. Before attaching the band, though, apply epoxy to the canoe's forward edge to seal the planks and stem tightly together. Af-

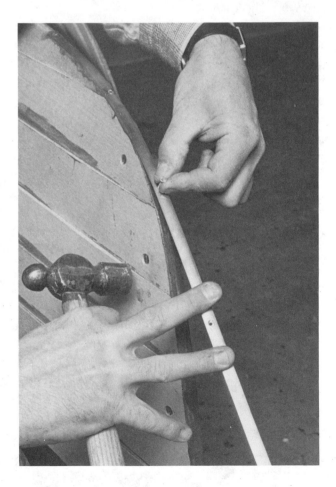

When nailing the stem band on a canoe, start on the garboard and work toward the sheer. Note the epoxy under the stem band, sealing the plank ends and stem tightly together.

ter a few minutes, follow with another application—a mixture of microballoons and epoxy. This brown putty fills any voids. To make the mix, fill a coffee can with about 1 ounce or one squirt of epoxy, then add a few tablespoons of microballoons, named thus because they are composed of millions of tiny beads, or "balloons." When these are added to the glue, the result is a medium-brown substance with the consistency of a fine chocolate sauce. Properly mixed, it pours like a thick maple syrup. Using a putty knife, apply the mix to the forward edge of the stem.

Then, starting at the keelson, drive 3/4-inch number 14 bronze ring nails through the holes in the band and into the stem's forward edge. Work down the stem while holding and bending the band around the curve. I push down on the band with the heel of my left hand, holding a nail with my left thumb and first finger, and swing the hammer with my right hand. Wipe away any excess putty.

The stem band end should fall 1/8 inch short of the sheer. This shortfall allows you to plane the rails without nicking your iron on the brass band.

Skiff Outer Stem

If you're building a skiff, you've already cut out rough stock for the inner and outer stems. The outer stem now attaches to the skiff's inner stem and planking.

Note that the planks extend past the inner stem (rough-cut). Trim these hood ends back to the stem profile with a plane, creating a flat leading edge, 3/4 inch wide, on the inner stem and hood ends. You must now "thickness," or plane, the outer stem, which was cut from 1 1/2-inch stock, to 3/4 inch. Plane the inner edge of the outer stem to make a good fit with the inner stem and hood ends. A spokeshave is the best tool for planing a curved surface.

Next, draw a centerline down the middle of the stem's outer edge. This line serves as a guide for placing the screws that will hold the outer stem in place. Use heavy wood screws, number 12s or 14s, usually about 3 inches long, and countersink them about 1/2 inch for plugs.

Then, before gluing, hold the outer stem in position and drive the screws in. The bottom edge of the stem will be flush with the keel (installed later). Make this dry fit carefully, and check the outer stem for alignment. To do this, place a bevel set on one side of the outer stem, then the other, checking the angles formed by the stem and planks. If the angles are equal, you know the stem is on straight. Some slight additional planing of the inside stem and hood ends or the inside edge of the outer stem may be necessary.

Once you're sure the outer stem fits perfectly, take it off, apply glue, reposition, and again drive fasteners to hold the stem permanently.

Rails (Outwales) Continued

At this point—whether you're building a canoe or a skiff—you're ready to return to the rails. Apply glue to both the sheerplanks and to the outwales. Align the rails to the sheerlines and hold them with spring clamps temporarily. Then add C-clamps, working from the center to the ends.

If necessary, loosen a clamp, adjust the rails, then retighten to achieve a fair sheerline. Carefully examine the rails from above and below, searching for spots where they might not touch the planks. If you discover such places, sometimes indicated by an inch-long slit of light shining through, reposition or add additional clamps.

In skiffs, the outwales are secured to the outer stem and the transom. At the bow, cut a compound bevel in the rail so that it butts to the outer stem, then fasten the rail with a number 8 wood screw, countersunk and bunged. At the stern, drive a number 8 wood screw through the rail (also slightly countersunk and bunged) and into the transom.

In canoes, I secure the rails to the stems with a countersunk number 8 wood screw. Be sure to offset opposing screws slightly so that they don't make contact after penetrating the

Dry-fit the outer stem of the skiff in place with screws in order to check its alignment before fastening it permanently.

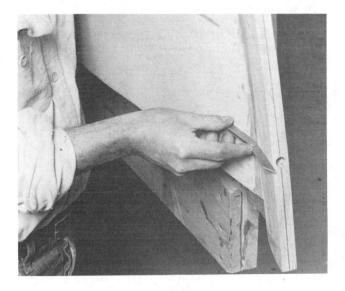

On both sides of the skiff's outer stem, use a bevel set to check alignment. If the stem is not on straight, slightly plane the hood ends or the inside edge of the outer stem.

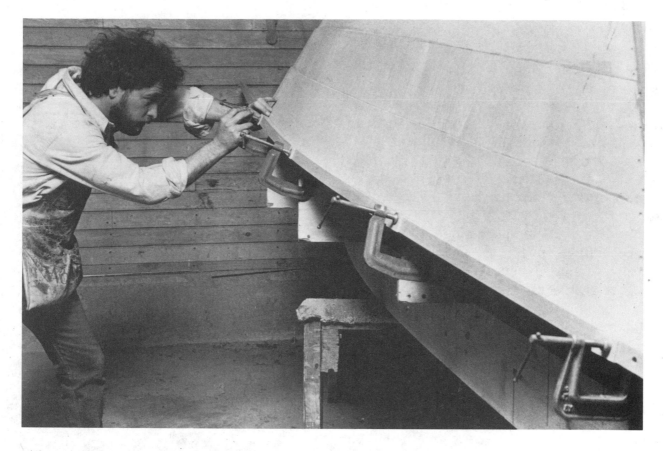

After applying glue to the outwale and the sheer plank of the skiff or canoe, clamp the rail at each station mold, then add more clamps, aligning and adjusting as you go.

Time spent making a good fit between the forward end of the outwale and the skiff's outer stem is time well spent. This is a highly visible joint, and it requires a compound bevel.

stem. Fill the holes with bungs, so that when you're through, your canoe will have very few visible fasteners. Cut the bungs with a plug cutter.

With one outwale secured, trim off the ends about ⅛ inch proud of the stem bands. That leaves you a little room to maneuver during the final shaping of the rails at the bow and stern. After securing one outwale, proceed to the other side of the canoe and do the other.

In about 30 minutes, the glue becomes rubbery. By then, any excess along the rails can be removed with a putty knife. Do this before the glue dries and hardens. Apply epoxy thickened with microballoons on voids and in screw holes at the stems.

Before taking your skiff or canoe off the jig, wait for it to dry, then sand it. Smooth the plywood, and add a slightly rounded edge to the planks' bottom edges. Smooth any putty.

By rounding the plank edges, you reduce your chances of catching an edge with a sander and causing a tear-out. In addition, paint adheres better to rounded edges than to sharp ones.

It's much easier to sand when the boat is fastened to the jig. Now is also a good time to put on your first coat of paint (see Chapter 10). I sand with a 4 x 4 vibrator sander, starting with 80- or 100-grit and progressing to 180- to 220-grit, as described in Chapter 10. Be careful. The planking veneers are thin. If you sand 4-millimeter plywood excessively on both sides, you'll end up with 2-millimeter plywood. Sand lightly.

With sanding completed, ask a friend to help you take your boat off the jig. If you're building a skiff, you can lift it off carefully, turn it right side up, and place it on sawhorses. If you're building a canoe, crawl beneath your jig and release the screws holding the canoe to the backbone. Nearby, set up two sawhorses with cross slings that will hold the canoe upright. Again, lift the canoe off the jig carefully. At this moment, the canoe is vulnerable. If you twist it off the jig hastily, you may accidentally split a plank off the stem at the sheer.

To make a sling-type sawhorse, suspend a piece of carpeting between the uprights. It's almost impossible to do the remaining work if the canoe is rocking on top of sawhorses with flat crosspieces. I place all my clamps and sometimes extra weights into the bottom of the canoe to increase its stability while I'm working on it in the sling-type sawhorses.

With the boat sitting upright, plane off the excess sheer planking flush to the rail. Also, trim off any excess stem length on a canoe with a backsaw.

Breasthooks

Shaping a breasthook is an important step. Few things show a boatbuilder's skill more readily than a neat-fitting breasthook, so spend the time to get it right.

Breasthook Blank. I make breasthooks with stock of various thicknesses, but in all cases the blank, or rough-cut breasthook, should be ¼ inch thicker than the rails. When first installed, the breasthook should rise ¼ inch above the sheerline so that you can later plane a crown on it, and its bottom edge should be flush with the bottom edges of the rails. My canoe breasthooks are 1 inch thick; for skiffs, they are 1¼ inches.

As an example, for canoes, I start with a piece of wood measuring, say, 6 by 12 inches (dimensions vary, of course, depending upon design requirements). At one end, I measure in ¾ inch from an edge and make a mark. At the other end, I measure in ¾ inch from the opposite edge and make another mark. Connecting these two marks creates a diagonal line across the surface of the piece. Then I saw along the diagonal and plane smooth the cut surfaces of the two triangle-shaped pieces. I then cut the third piece, a centerpiece of the same thickness as the triangles and ⅜ inch wide. With the centerpiece, you eliminate a short-grain-to-short-grain glue joint.

To secure the three pieces during gluing requires a jig made from scrap wood. Cut a piece of plywood slightly larger than all three pieces, then add two cleats to the surface. Before gluing, dry-fit the breasthook into the jig. Next, cut two long, narrow wedges to fit neatly between the breasthook and the cleats.

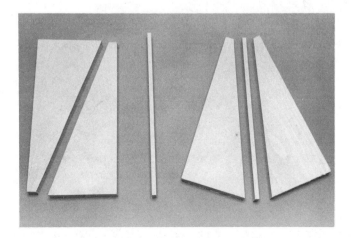

*To make a breasthook for a skiff or canoe, slice a piece of stock diagonally (**left**), and cut a centerpiece. Then position the pieces (**right**), and glue them together.*

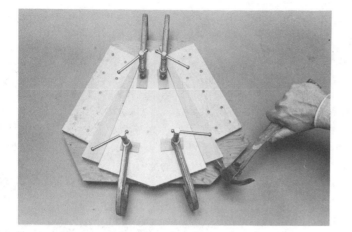

*After applying glue, wedge the breasthook blank
into a jig made of a plywood base
and plywood cleats.*

Lay a small sheet of clear plastic over the jig so that the breasthook won't stick to it during gluing. Apply glue to the edges of the triangles and to both sides of the centerpiece. Insert the breasthook into the jig, hold it down with C-clamps, and drive the wedges in so that they fit tightly, forcing the three pieces together. Clean off excess glue before the breasthook dries.

After drying, you have a breasthook blank, a diamond-shaped piece of wood. Cut this piece square across on both its forward and after ends, plane off any excess glue, and smooth the surfaces. To avoid confusion later on when building a canoe, label the breast-hook according to its intended location. Pick the side that looks the best for the top, and mark the bottom with a *B* if the breasthook is for the bow, or an *S* if for the stern.

Fitting the Breasthook. Center the blank on top of the rails, and align the breasthook's ³/₈-inch-wide centerpiece over the exact centerline of the boat. Holding the blank centered with one hand, with your other hold a pencil stub that's been carved flat on one side. (Make the stub not longer than 2 inches so that it fits snugly against the sheerplank.) Draw an outline on the underside of the breasthook blank,

moving the pencil along the inside of the sheer planks on both sides and along the stem.

Saw out this shape, cutting a little proud, then plane it smooth, leaving half the line. You now have a triangular piece of wood that doesn't yet fit into the peak, because the stem and sheerplanks angle aft and inward, respectively, from top to bottom, while the edges of the breasthook blank are still square.

Using a bevel set, copy the angle of the stem onto the forward edge of the breasthook blank. To do this, lay a straightedge flat across the rails, just aft of the stem. Position the bevel set against the stem and straightedge, then transfer the angle taken from the stem onto both sides of the forward end of the breasthook. Connect the two lines across the bottom, and across the top of the breasthook, about ¹/₁₆ inch in from the forward edge, cut a shallow scribe mark with a knife. The scribe mark eliminates the chance of tear-outs when you are beveling the forward edge.

With a block plane or rasp, make the bevel on the forward edge keeping in mind that shaping a breasthook is a cut-and-fit operation all the way. Once the forward bevel has been cut, you must bevel the sides to fit tightly to the planking. There's more than one way to transfer the angle from the planks to the sides of the breasthook, but I do it by eyeing the gaps at the forward and after edges of the breasthook. Then I turn the blank over and trace lines indicating those gap widths onto the bottom edges. Finally, I add additional reference lines parallel with and as close as possible to the upper side edges of the breast-hook.

Place the breasthook in a vise and plane the sides, starting at the bottom lines (the winding bevel lines) and working slowly back toward the top edges. Plane with the grain and repeatedly check to see how the breasthook fits. If it becomes too narrow, remove some wood from the front bevel where the breast-hook touches the stem. Never plane off your pencil lines; they are your references.

Tabs. Now you're ready to add details to

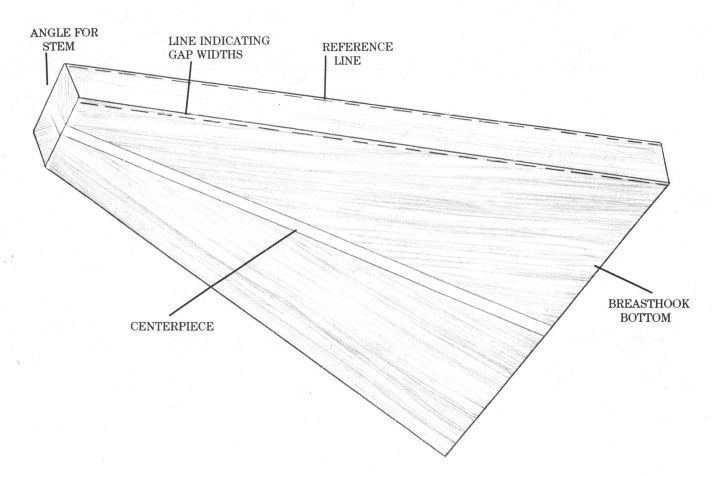

ANGLE FOR
STEM

LINE INDICATING
GAP WIDTHS

REFERENCE
LINE

CENTERPIECE

BREASTHOOK
BOTTOM

When beveling the breasthook's sides, you can use reference lines and lines indicating gap widths to check your progress.

the breasthook, beginning with the two trailing ends where the inwales land. I call these tabs. They are as wide as the spacer blocks between the planking and the inwales, usually $3/8$ to $1/2$ inch.

Measure in from one side of the breasthook, at the aft edge, a distance equal to the width of the spacer blocks. Hold a spacer block flush to the outside edge of the breasthook, and draw a line $1\frac{1}{2}$ inches long parallel with the breasthook side. (Beware: This line represents the top edge of the tab, not the bottom edge. Because of the hull flare, the tab is a parallelogram in cross section, with bottom and top edges staggered. You'll need extra wood on the inside face so you can cut the hull flare into the outside face.) Obviously,

this operation has to be done on both sides of the breasthook.

Forty-five Degree Cut. Now you need to mark a pencil line with a 45-degree angle at the forward end of the $1\frac{1}{2}$-inch-long line. The new line represents the 45-degree angle cut on the end of the inwale. To determine the length of these lines on the breasthook, lay a combination square flat across the top of a piece of inwale stock at a 45-degree angle. Measure the diagonal distance, and transfer this distance to your breasthook along each of the 45-degree lines, adding $1/4$ inch as a margin for error.

The next step is to connect the ends of the angled lines with a curve. To do this, I simply

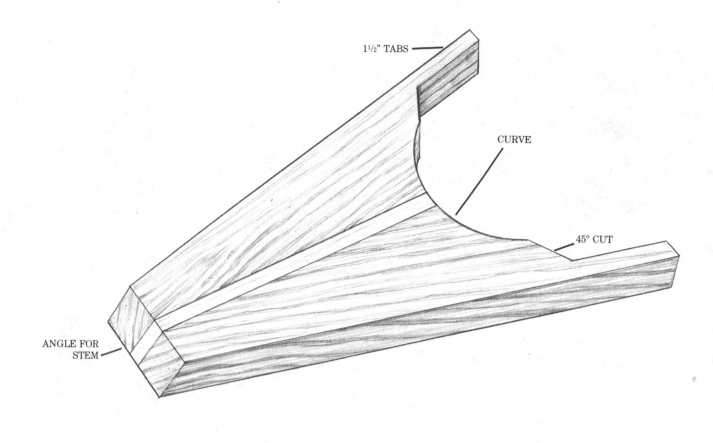

1½" TABS

CURVE

45° CUT

ANGLE FOR
STEM

Inverted breasthook showing tabs, 45-degree angle cuts, angle for stem, and curve.

take a coffee can or any perfectly round shape and trace along its edge. Whatever looks good to you works fine here. Once I have drawn my curve, I rough-cut the tabs, the 45-degree angles, and the curve with a band saw or jigsaw. Remember, the tabs form parallelograms, so you need to cut proud of the 1½-inch lines.

Your breasthook is now ready to be installed permanently. Apply glue to all surfaces. Drive two number 8 wood screws through each outwale and into the breasthook. Countersink the screws and fill the holes with plugs. Hold the breasthook tabs with C-clamps and clamp pads. After the glue dries, remove the clamps and plane the crown. I like a crown of about ³/₁₆ inch, but yours may vary.

Spacer Blocks

Spacer blocks lie between the inwales and sheerplanks, and must now be cut out of the extra rail that was rough-cut earlier. I make the blocks about 3¼ inches long and space them evenly between the bow and stern. This can be done either mathematically or with a spacer template; for me, using a template is easier.

After marking placement positions for each block, I apply glue to the blocks and planks, and secure each block in place with C-clamps and pads. Place the blocks flush with the top of the sheer. Due to the flare of the boat, the inboard edges of the blocks will be slightly proud of the sheer, but this is nothing to worry about.

Skiff Quarter Knees

These connect the sides of the boat to the transom. Whenever possible, I make them from applewood knees, the grain in which "turns the corner," allowing me to fasten through the transom and planking into edge grain. The best place to find these bent pieces is in apple orchards after pruning. A less satisfactory, but often necessary, choice is a straight-grain quarter knee, which can be fastened only by driving screws through a short grain. Some plans call for plywood quarter knees.

Quarter knees may be installed in various ways:

1. They may be attached with a trailing tab nearly identical to the tab on the breasthook. The tab has the same width and thickness as the spacer block, and it serves as a

Flapjack's quarter knees fasten to the inwales and transom.

"landing point" for the inwale. The quarter knee fastens to the transom and sheerplank.

2. They may be attached to the transom and inwale, the inwale butting to the transom. (Steve Redmond uses this technique for the Flapjack.)

3. They may be attached in either one of the first two ways, but built from bent, laminated strips. With this quarter knee, you avoid driving screws through a short grain, but cutting and laminating the separate pieces is time-consuming.

I prefer the first option because the quarter knees attach directly to the transom and sheerplanks, and I think this looks the best.

Fitting a quarter knee, a painstaking task, requires steps similar to those for the breasthook. Take your time. First, copy the angle of the sheerstrake to the transom, then bevel the quarter knee to fit against the transom. You may need to bevel the side of the quarter knee that attaches to the sheerstrake to allow the after edge of the quarter knee to land on the transom. Apply glue and fasten each quarter knee with wood screws.

Rails (Inwales) Continued

To install the inwales, you must first do some more work on the breasthook. Because you made the breasthook tabs a bit proud, you must now trim them with a chisel to the exact thickness of the spacer blocks. With a straightedge, draw lines, of the same width as the spacer blocks, along the inside edges of the 1½-inch-long cuts. You may use spacer blocks to draw the lines. Then draw another line just inside and as close as possible to each of the 45-degree cuts.

With a razor-sharp chisel, pare along the tab edge and the 45-degree edge, trying to create smooth, flat surfaces for the inwale to land on.

Take a bevel set and transfer the breasthook's 45-degree angle onto the forward end of the inwale. After trimming, the breasthook angles may have been altered slightly, so it's important to transfer the actual angles with a

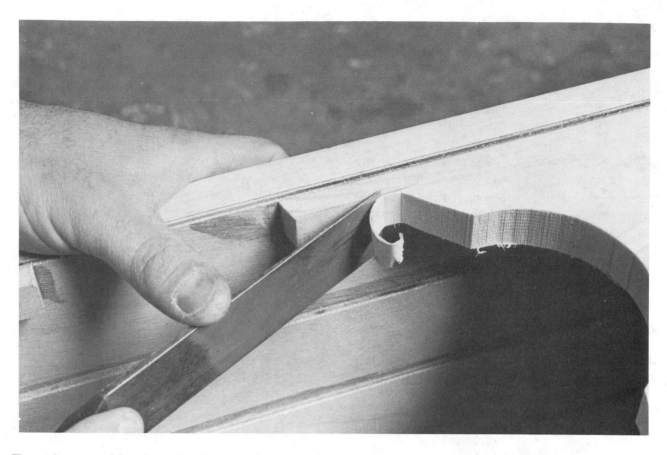

To make a good landing for the inwale, pare along the breasthook's tab edge with a sharp chisel.

bevel set, rather than simply cutting off the inwales at 45 degrees.

Just as the breasthook's 45-degree cut may not have been precisely 45 degrees, neither is the edge of the cut precisely square to the upper surface of the breasthook. The bottom of the inwale must therefore be slightly longer than the top, and you must bevel the end of the inwale to achieve this. Lay the bevel set on top of the tab at the apex of the 45-angle. Copy and transfer this vertical angle onto the inwale. You now have a compound angle drawn on the inwale, and are ready to cut.

Cut the compound bevel with a backsaw, and smooth it with a chisel. Dry-fit the end of the rail into the breasthook's 45-degree angle. If necessary, keep trimming the rail until the end fits precisely. You won't have the same opportunity at the boat's opposite end. There, the fit must be perfect the first time, unless you make the first cut long, then whittle the end down.

Once you have one end that fits neatly, clamp it up dry (without gluing). Working from bow to stern, clamp the inwale at every spacer block, using C-clamps and protective pads. (If you don't clamp it at every spacer block, the rail will inevitably end up short when you glue it.) Stop when you reach a point about 2 feet from the stern.

Now you're ready to mark the other end of the rail with another compound bevel, so that it too will fit neatly. If you're building a canoe, you want the end of the inwale to fit in the 45-degree angle on the aft breasthook, while for skiffs, it can either butt to the transom or land on the tab of a quarter knee. In either case, you can adapt and use the following steps as a guide.

1. To make the inwale fit to a breasthook, quarter knee, or transom, you need either a 2-foot rule or a stick of at least that length. Come back an arbitrary distance from the apex of the 45-degree angle in the breasthook

After a 45-degree angle in the breasthook has been cleaned up with a chisel, it may not be exactly 45 degrees, so recheck with a bevel set.

Transfer the exact shape of the nominal 45-degree angle, as measured with the bevel set, onto the rail.

When you have cut the compound bevel in the inwale end, dry-fit it into the breasthook's 45-degree angle.

or quarter knee, say, about 2 feet. Make a tick mark on a spacer block, and transfer it onto the inwale.

2. Hold your 2-foot rule on the mark just made on the rail and go back the same distance, making another mark on the rail. This will be the apex of the 45-degree angled cut on the inwale to fit into the breasthook, quarter knee, or transom.

3. Like the cut at the other end of the rail, this is a compound bevel. Measure the horizontal and vertical components of the bevel as at the other end, and transfer these to the inwale. Then cut the bevel so that the end fits neatly into the breasthook, quarter knee, or transom. All this can be done while the rails are clamped up.

As I mentioned, if you want to play it safe,

you can cut the rail a bit long, then whittle it back until it fits. To avoid marring the surface of the breasthook, quarter knee, or transom, place a piece of scrap wood over it while cutting bevels in the rails.

Once compound bevels have been cut on both ends, you're ready to glue the inwales. Apply glue to the entire inner surface of the inwales, not just to places that touch the breasthooks and spacer blocks. Behind the inwales is a difficult place to paint, so a little extra glue won't do any harm; it adds a protective coating. Start at one end and work toward the other. As before, secure the inwales with C-clamps and pads. For Flapjack skiffs, screws are also driven through the inwales, at the spacer blocks. Screws are not necessary when you are fastening inwales in a canoe.

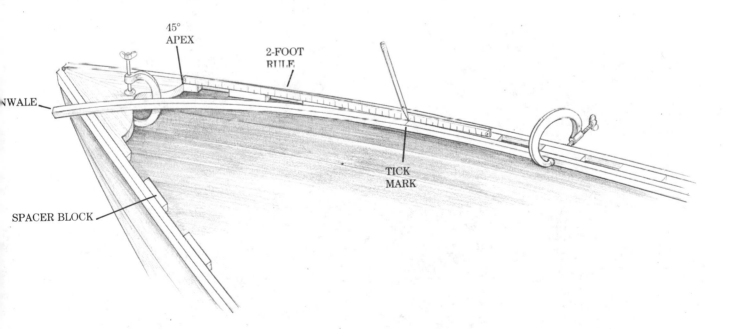

45°
APEX

2-FOOT
RULE

INWALE

TICK
MARK

SPACER BLOCK

To measure the second end of the inwale to the precise length needed to fit into the breasthook (canoe) or quarter knee or transom (skiff), you must first make a tick mark on a spacer block about 2 feet from the end, then transfer it to the inwale.

Gluing and clamping an inwale.

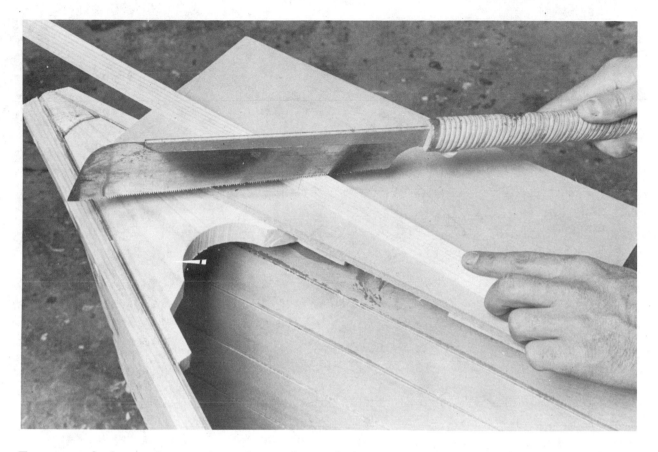

To protect the boat, place a piece of scrap beneath the rail when you make the compound cut.

Skiffs

Shaping the Outer Stem

To shape a skiff's outer stem, mark concave curves using a rounded edge, such as a can, on either side of the piece. Boat plans may show the exact placement of the curves; often, they begin at the bottom of the sheer planks, as in the drawing on page 81. Cut the scallop on either side by grinding it out with a disk sander. For the Flapjack, I shape the outer stem below the scallops so that it tapers 1/8 inch on each side to a thickness of 1/2 inch along the leading edge. The stem remains rectangular above the scallops.

Keel and Skeg

Keels vary in construction, as indicated in the plans for a boat. The Flapjack's keel has a rectangular midsection, tapering in width toward the stem and transom, and can be cut from 3/4-inch-thick oak or mahogany. Rough-cut the keel stock 1 inch longer than the boat bottom, leaving this excess for initial shaping.

After cutting a piece of stock for the keel, place it on the bottom of the boat. Next, draw a lengthwise centerline, then draw two lines across the keel to indicate the forward and after edges of the centerboard trunk. The section between the two lines remains rectangular, while the keel segments forward and aft of the trunk are tapered.

Mark the forward taper on either side of the keel, laying a straightedge between the line representing the forward end of the centerboard trunk and the outside edge of the outer stem or cutwater. The aft end of the keel outline tapers back to the transom according to plan specifications. Once the tapers are drawn, cut them out with a jigsaw, then plane

To sharpen the entrance of a skiff's outer stem (cutwater), grind out a curve and plane a taper.

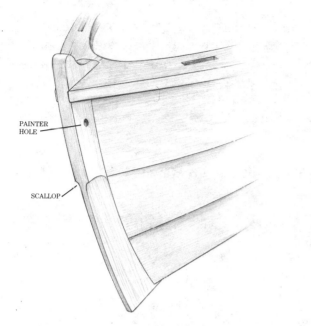

A finished outer stem, showing the taper from the curve to the bottom. Add a painter hole as shown.

the edges smooth. Reposition the keel on the bottom of the boat so that the keel's centerline aligns with the centerlines on the transom and outer stem. Also, be sure to center the keel amidships, with its edges equidistant from the centerline.

You must now cut a bevel on the keel's forward end so that it will fit neatly behind the outer stem. Transfer the angle from the outer stem to the forward end of the keel with a bevel set, then cut this angle.

Once you have a good fit at the forward end and can center the keel, hold it down with heavy weights and trace its edges to create a full keel pattern on the plywood bottom.

With the keel on the boat bottom, measure in from the transom the length of the skeg, (taking this length from the plans) and mark this distance. Then outline a slot of the same thickness as the skeg. Remove the keel, and cut out the slot with a jigsaw.

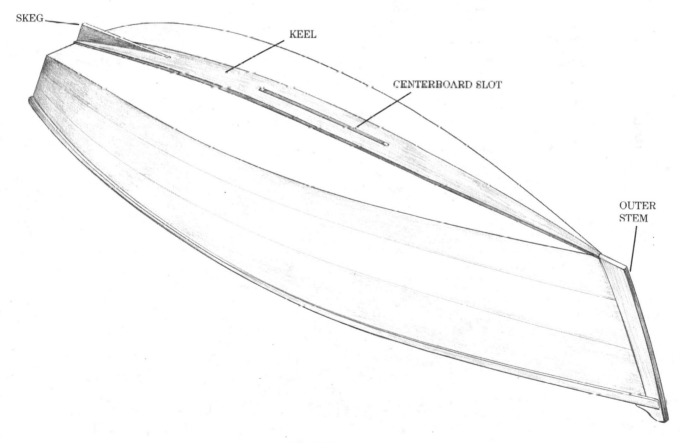

A skiff with bottom complete.

About ¾ inch inside and all along the edge of the drawn keel outline, drill small holes through the bottom approximately on 8-inch centers. These pilot holes will guide you, when you crawl beneath your jig and drive screws up through the bottom and into the keel. Be sure to position the pilot holes so that screws won't interfere with the centerboard slot.

Dry-fit the keel on the bottom, and hold it down with screws at four evenly spaced places. Work from stem to stern to avoid bulges. At this point, you want the keel to stay on and bend with the boat's rocker. With the keel secured this way, you're ready to fit the skeg.

Skeg. Cut out a rectangular piece of stock,

Marking the bottom curve on the skeg blank.

¾ inch thick, making it 1 inch wider and ½ inch longer than the finished skeg dimensions. To keep this blank oriented, draw an arrow at the forward edge of the stock, pointing toward the bow.

Fit the blank into the slot, and trace a line, using the top edge of the keel as a guide, along the blank. That line, which corresponds to the curve of the bottom, now denotes the bottom edge of the skeg. Once you've traced it, remove the skeg blank and cut along the line with either a band saw or jigsaw.

Now place the blank back into the slot, and position a 2-foot square so that its long leg rests on the transom and crosses the skeg (see the accompanying photograph). Extend a line from the top edge of the keel across the skeg, thus denoting the skeg's after edge.

The aft edge of the skeg has the same angle as the transom.

From the plan, get the depth of the skeg along its after edge, and make a corresponding mark on the blank. Then place a straightedge from that mark to the forward end of the skeg, and draw a line connecting these two points.

Remove the blank, and cut along both lines. Plane and chamfer the edges. Your skeg is complete.

Installing the Keel and Skeg

You are now ready to install the keel and skeg permanently. First, loosen the four screws holding the keel temporarily. Apply glue to the keel and bottom. Center the keel and hold it down with heavy weights. Go beneath the jig, and, starting at the bow and working toward the stern, drive screws up through the pilot holes and into the keel.

Drill about four to six evenly spaced pilot holes into the skeg slot. Apply glue to the skeg and bottom, and drive screws up through the plywood bottom and into the skeg. (The centerline on the inside bottom can also serve as a guide when you are drilling holes for the skeg.) I use $1\frac{1}{2}$-inch number 10 wood screws. Yours could be heavier or lighter, depending upon the size of the skeg. Wipe off excess epoxy. Once the glue has dried, chamfer the square edges of the keel.

Centerboard and Centerboard Trunk

For a sailing version of the Flapjack, I make the centerboard trunk from $\frac{1}{2}$-inch mahogany plywood and two $\frac{3}{4}$- by 1-inch mahogany end logs, about 12 inches long. The end logs are spacers that pass through the boat bottom and, until trimmed (which you can do at any convenient time), protrude several inches beyond it. I make the Flapjack's centerboard of $\frac{3}{4}$-inch mahogany plywood. To compensate for swelling, warping, and the

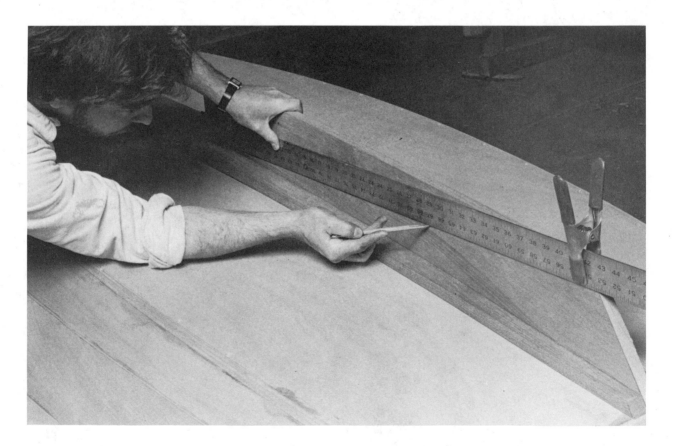

Marking out the skeg on the boat saves time.

Plane and chamfer the skeg edges.

possibility of fouling, centerboards are always narrower than the trunk opening.

First, cut out the two sides of the trunk. These need to be rough-cut taller than their final height so that they can be trimmed later to conform to the rocker of the boat bottom and their tops made parallel with the waterline. At the ends of these trunk pieces, draw lines representing the ¾-inch thickness of the end logs.

Next, draw and cut out the plywood centerboard. At the pivot end of the centerboard, using a compass, draw a half-circle with a diameter equaling the board width. The pivot point of the compass will become the pivot point of the board. Attach a piece of string at this point, and at the opposite end of the string, attach a pencil and swing an arc to draw a radius tangent to the free end of the board. The centerboard end must have a radius cut so that it can fall freely from the trunk.

Place one side of the centerboard trunk directly on top of the other, then place the

centerboard on top of the trunk sides, resting it just as it would be if it were retracted in the trunk. Center it between the two end log lines

Centerboard trunk sides with the two end logs projecting from the bottom. These end logs are cut long initially to protrude through the bottom of the skiff, then trimmed flush when convenient.

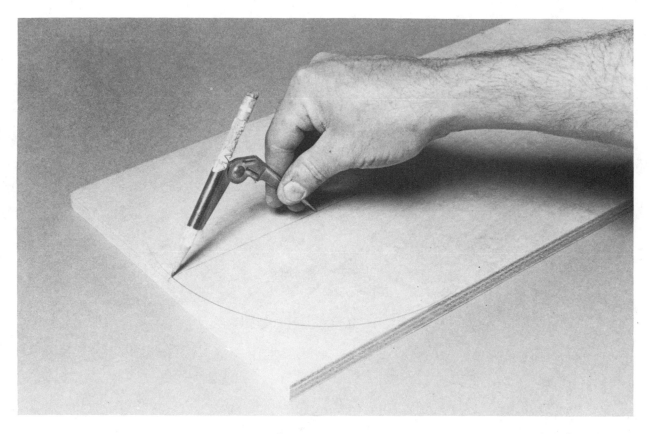

Tracing the pivot end of the centerboard. The pivot point for the compass is also the pivot point for the centerboard.

drawn on the trunk sides, and leave its top edge about ¹/₂ inch below the top edge of the

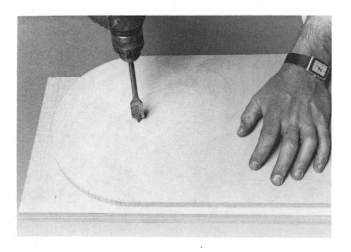

Carefully align the centerboard atop the trunk sides, then drill a bolt hole. The line marking the end log position, visible at the left, serves as a guide.

trunk. At the pivot point for the centerboard, drill a bolt hole through all three pieces.

At this stage, ream out the centerboard's hole with a rat-tail rasp so that the board will pivot freely on the bolt. If you were to keep the same size bolt hole in the centerboard, the swelling of the centerboard might prevent the board from pivoting.

To shape the bottom of the centerboard trunk so that it conforms with the rocker, hold a trunk side in position, then, slide a slightly elevated pencil (held on a small wood block) along the bottom of the boat to trace the curve onto the bottom of the trunk side. Cut this curve out of both panels at the same time, and plane the bottom edges square to the sides while they're clamped together.

Apply epoxy, which perhaps offers more protection than paint, to the insides of the trunk. These surfaces are difficult to reach once the trunk is permanently in place. Then glue and screw the trunk sides to the end logs.

Slide a slightly elevated pencil along the bottom to trace the boat's rocker. If your boat has extreme rocker, you may need a small block beneath the pencil.

Next, refer to your plan and mark the appropriate centerboard trunk slot length and width on the inside of the boat. Climb inside the boat and drill a hole through the slot area, making it large enough for a jigsaw blade, then saw out the slot. Alternatively, make a plunge cut with a circular saw.

Lower the assembled centerboard trunk into position to see how it fits. If the end logs won't squeeze through the slot, I widen it with a rasp, but a tight fit is best. Glue and clamp the trunk in place.

Now add caps to each end of the trunk, and bed logs to the lower sides. Bed logs are like cleats; these heavy-stock pieces help secure the trunk, which is subject to strong

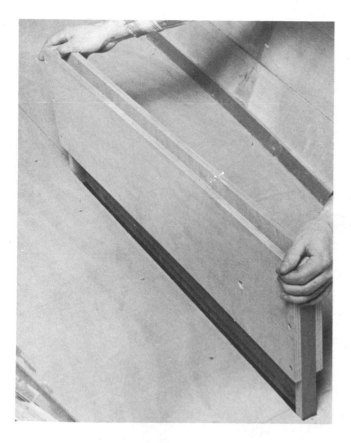

A snug centerboard fit is best.

twisting forces from the centerboard when the boat is under sail.

Refer to your plans, and shape the bed logs the same way you shaped the bottom of the centerboard trunk. Once the bed logs conform to the boat's rocker, glue them to the sides of the trunk and to the bottom. Then drive screws through them and into the keel.

The end caps are two pieces of stock, wide enough and tall enough to cover the two ends of the trunk. I fasten these with glue and wood screws.

Lead Casting. You must add lead to weigh down the centerboard, and you might apply some ingenuity to obtaining this lead as cheaply as possible. I pick up scrap lead from gas stations, which sell or give away old lead weights used to balance automobile tires.

When casting, use extreme care. Molten lead can spatter violently if it contacts moisture.

Avoid casting lead in wet or green woods. Once, I accidentally overheated some lead and

Sometimes Pop needs a little help.

One bed log and one end cap in position on the trunk. The top of the end log is visible behind the end cap. Wood screws hold better when a tapered drill bit is used. Fuller bits, which are tapered and have an attached countersink, can be ordered from Jamestown Distributors (address in Appendix).

poured it into a centerboard. The accompanying photo shows the results. Work outdoors or in well-ventilated spaces to avoid inhaling toxic fumes. Always wear heavy clothing, safety goggles, gloves, and a respirator. Thick leather clothes offer good protection.

For the lead weight, make a hole near the centerboard bottom of the size indicated on the plans. To make the lead adhere, drive about four or five 1-inch ring nails into the hole's inner edge. Then, lay the centerboard flat on a table-saw top and clamp it down. Any steel-topped table or flat metal surface will do. Make sure the centerboard is level.

Don't overheat the lead for the centerboard. The piece at the right shows what can happen when you do.

Nails driven in the hole help secure the lead.

I melt the lead over a propane-fired burner, first placing about 15 pounds of scrap lead into an old steel cooking pot, then turning on the flame. After 15 to 20 minutes, the lead turns into a silvery liquid. If any scrap metal pieces float to the surface, I skim them off with an old spoon attached to a stick extension-handle.

As soon as the lead is molten—and no later—I carefully pour it into the centerboard hole to about 1/8 inch over the top of the hole. Lead solidifies quickly, but it also retains heat for at least 30 minutes, so resist the temptation to touch the lead. Leave it alone to cool.

Once the lead cools, plane any rough surfaces or edges flush with the plywood. When it is smooth, chamfer and round all plywood edges and give the centerboard an airfoil shape as drawn in the plans. Then paint it entirely with epoxy.

Seats

Cutting, fitting, and installing seats requires precision joinerwork. Here, you become a furniture maker. Exactness is a must. To help avoid confusion, I label all pieces. For example, an aft cleat for the aft seat on the port side would be marked "PA." I often use 3/4-inch-thick mahogany for seats, and if they are to be finished bright, I make sure the upper faces have the prettiest grain.

Forward Seat. The 11-inch-wide forward seat of the Flapjack skiff crosses the centerboard trunk and attaches to the sides of the hull with cleats. From your plans, you can locate and mark the seat's forward and after edges, with a square, across the top of the centerboard trunk. To determine the seat length, I measure the inside hull width with a story pole, two pointed sticks that slide back and forth next to each other (also called slipsticks). For this job, the story pole is ideal. A tape measure is difficult to hold and too floppy for accurate measurements across the hull.

Let the story pole straddle the trunk, and

Wear protective clothing when working with lead.

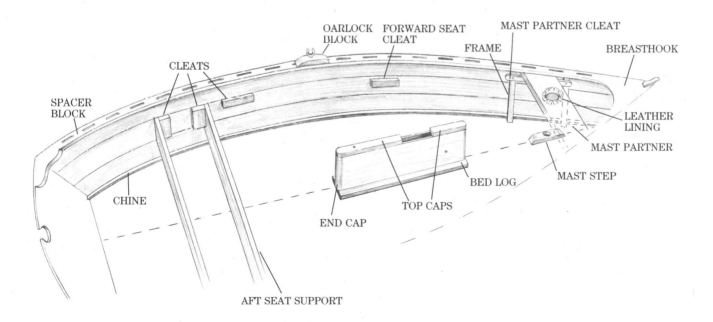

Skiff interior, showing joinerwork.

Forward seat. Note that at this stage chamfering has not been done, and the support cleats have not been installed.

Use a story pole to measure hull widths, and as a straightedge when copying bevels.

slide the sticks apart until the pointed edges touch the sides of the hull. Make marks where the points touch the planking, then clamp the sticks together with a spring clamp. With the pole extended, you can determine the length of the forward and after edges of the seat, and transfer these distances to the seat stock. At each end of the stock, connect the marks, creating cut lines.

Now you need to bevel the ends of the seat so that it fits inside the hull. Hold a straightedge such as the story pole across the centerboard trunk, and copy the bevel between the planking and the bottom edge of the straightedge. Transfer this bevel onto the seat, cut it, and plane it smooth.

Use the same bevel for the cleats that support the seat. After cutting the bevels, I hold each cleat in its proper position and check to see if it needs shaping. Plane the side of the cleat that meets the planking to achieve a good fit to the curve of the hull. If you don't do this, you may cinch in a plank, creating an unfair flat spot, when you attach the cleat with glue and screws.

Once the cleat is beveled and shaped, reposition it and trace its outline with a pencil. Then remove it, drill three pilot holes through the hull, again reposition it, and drill three slightly countersunk holes from the outside. Then fasten the cleat.

Check the seat to make sure it fits, but don't install it permanently because it will interfere with sanding and painting. As a general rule, I find it's easier and more effective to finish seats and other parts outside the boat, before they are installed. When you do fasten the seat, drive two 1¼-inch number 10 wood screws through each end of the board and into the cleats. Countersink the screws only slightly, because deep holes catch water, and you want to avoid using bungs here so that you can remove the seat for refinishing.

Before chamfering the seat edges (and after measuring for the aft seat, see following section), shape and fit the top caps. These two pieces of wood lie on top of the centerboard trunk on either side of the seat, and are fastened with glue and screws. Once the caps and seats are installed, you can chamfer all the edges. On the seat edges, make a stop chamfer (a chamfer with a transition into a square edge) on either side of the centerboard trunk. Use a spokeshave for the stop chamfer.

Aft Seat. On many small skiffs, aft seats are made of slats placed across supports. For the Flapjack I built for this book, however, I was lucky enough to find a 21-inch-wide, ¾-inch-thick piece of mahogany, from which I shaped the seats.

To allow for the swelling and shrinking of large boards, I fasten them with screws driven through oversized holes. Always compensate for the movement of wood. In general, boards swell and shrink up to ¼ inch per foot of width.

Steve Redmond, who designed the Flapjack, positioned the aft seat relatively far forward for optimum load distribution. In this lightweight, well-rockered boat, balance is critical for proper sailing and rowing performance.

When installing seats, you want them all level. To do this on the Flapjack, I take my 8-foot-long steel straightedge and place it lengthwise on top of the centerboard trunk; the lower edge of the straightedge then gives me the correct height for the top edges of the aft seat supports. These two supports span the width of the boat and attach to the sides of the hull.

To determine the length of the supports, again place the story pole across the hull, and transfer that length to the seat support stock. Transfer and mark bevels, then cut the supports, following procedures similar to those used for the forward seat.

Lay the supports inside the hull in the correct positions, and trace around their ends with a pencil. Drive three pilot holes out through the hull inside each tracing, then mount the supports temporarily by driving three screws from the outside, through the planking and into the end grain of each support. (These screw heads will be puttied over

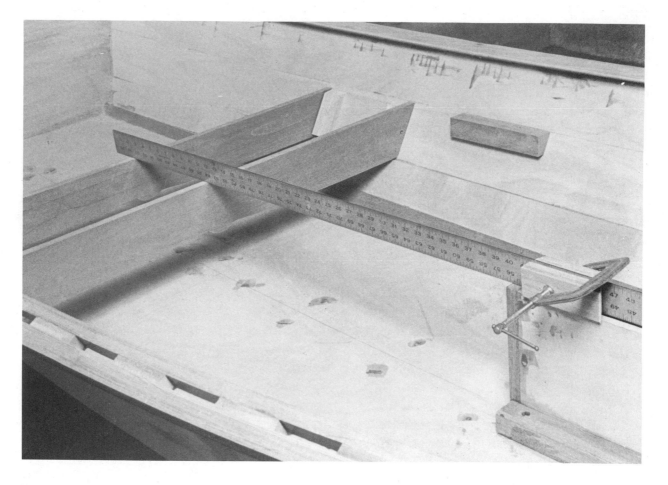

The forward and aft seats of the Flapjack skiff should be at the same height.

later, when you paint.) The end grain isn't strong enough to hold the seat supports permanently, so I add cleats between the supports, securing these to the planking with glue and screws, then driving screws through the supports and into the cleats.

On some small skiffs, as mentioned, the aft seats are made of several fore-and-aft slats, spaced at least 1/8 inch apart to allow for expansion. I position the slats over the supports and draw two straight lines across the tops of all the slats, indicating where to drive screws.

Drive wood screws through the slats and into the supports, but do not glue the slats to the supports. You'll want to remove them later for refinishing. If you like, countersink the screw holes, then fill them with bungs. I dip the bungs in varnish, not glue, so that they too can be removed easily.

Oarlocks

On the Flapjack, oarlocks are positioned about 12 inches aft of the aft edge of the forward seat, with about 6 inches from the top of the seat to the bottom of the oarlock horn.

I use bronze oarlocks with either side mounts or sockets, screwed into a shaped block about 8 inches long and wide enough to cover the rails. Rough-cut the blocks with a jigsaw or band saw, and follow up by smoothing and rounding them with a spokeshave. The exact dimensions of the blocks can be scaled off the plans, but the shape (other than the height) is not critical.

Sculling Notch

A sculling notch in the transom comes in handy if you lose an oar and need to scull ashore. If you lose your rudder, you can steer with an oar in the notch. On a windless day, sculling is an enjoyable, easy way to move along.

I draw the notch by tracing outside the horn of a standard number 1 Wilcox Crittenden oarlock. Once I've traced the horn, I cut the notch out with a jigsaw, then smooth the cut and round the edges with a spokeshave.

Frames

There are four frames in this skiff, the function of which is to increase hull stiffness and strength immediately forward and aft of the mast partner. Each vertical frame is notched to fit the chines and planks; extending each notch slightly above the chine or plank shelf over which it fits creates a limber hole, allowing water to drain along the shelf.

The frames should stand perpendicular to the waterline; if they appear to be canted fore or aft, they will seem misplaced. Furthermore, cutting the notches is a bit tricky because you must compensate for the curve of the bow and the angle of the chines. To start, I cut a 3/4-inch-thick, 2½-inch-wide piece of mahogany the proper length to span the distance from the boat bottom to the underside of the inwale. Later, the frame will be cut about ⅛ inch short and its bottom end rounded so that it doesn't touch the boat bottom.

Position the aft frame pieces as shown on the plans. First, draw the notch for the chine and cut it out. Then, stand the frame in position against the planking, and trace a pencil line up along the frame, guiding it in your hand so that it follows the shapes and ridges of the planking. By doing this, you're copying the inside contour of the hull onto the framing

Draw notches for the frame piece by following the plank jogs with a pencil traveling on a thin block.

piece. Remember to extend the notches above the plank edges, creating limber holes. Round the bottom of the framing piece, and install it with glue and wood screws driven in from the outside through the planks.

Mast Partner

The mast partner provides lateral support to the mast at rail height. Get the width for the partner and its fore-and-aft position from your plans, then mark the rails where the mast partner will go. Rough-cut a piece of stock for the partner, position it over the rails, and mark its forward and aft edges to the correct lengths. Connect the marks and cut the board, creating a piece that roughly fits.

Next, bevel the board's ends. At each end, cut and plane both the top and side so that the partner fits flush to the underside of the rails and tight to the planks. To shape the ends correctly, transfer bevels from both the sides of the hull and the undersides of the rails—in that order.

Once the mast partner fits snugly beneath the rails, you can put it aside. Later, after making the mast (Chapter 9), cut a center hole in the mast partner and line it with leather. For a sprit rig, the mast shouldn't rattle around in the hole, but it needs to be loose enough so that it can turn easily. I fasten the partner to the rails and fasten support cleats underneath it, spanning the frames. The cleats sandwich the partner to the rails. I install the partner and cleats after painting or varnishing.

Mast Step

The mast step is a simple block similar to an oarlock block, with a center hole slightly bigger than the bottom end of the mast. Make the hole deep enough so the mast won't pop out easily. The mast step's position (on the plan) determines the rake of the mast. To fasten it, apply epoxy to the mating surfaces and drive wood screws down through the step and into the keel, countersinking and bunging them if you wish.

Final Details

After the partner is in and finishing work is complete, I add a belaying pin at the forward edge of the mast partner and a pad eye just aft of the mast hole. The pad eye is for the downhaul, and the belaying pin secures the halyard. I also install thumb cleats on top of the rails, one on either side in the stern. The mainsheet loops around these cleats. For the centerboard line, I fasten a cleat to the aft end cap of the centerboard trunk.

Canoes

Flooring

On my smaller canoes, the floor covers 2 feet of the bottom. Typically, I use a 24-inch-square piece of 4-millimeter mahogany plywood. For 14-foot canoes, the floor is 8 feet long; for 16-foot canoes, I make a 10-foot floor by butting together one 8-foot and two 1-foot pieces (one at either end, for symmetry) of plywood. In 14- and 16-foot canoes, the floor is wide enough to cover the garboards, while in solo canoes, the floor covers the garboards and broadstrakes. Once epoxied in place, the plywood floor adds strength and rigidity to the hull.

Here, I'll describe floor installation in an 11½-footer. To begin, cut a 24-inch-square panel of 4-millimeter plywood, and draw centerlines square across the piece in both directions, thus creating a grid for marking the widths of the canoe's bottom.

Next, find the exact fore-and-aft center of the boat, and mark a perpendicular line on the keelson with a combination square. Next to this centerline, note "CL." Now, measure aft from the centerline 14 inches, and mark another line square across the keelson, this line indicating the position for the thwart ("TL"). Then go 2 inches aft of this line and make a third perpendicular line marking the aft edge of the floor panel ("AL"). In this canoe, the thwart falls 14 inches aft of center, so the after edge of the floor is 16 inches aft of center.

The Flapjack skiff with, from bow to stern, the mast partner, forward seat, and aft seat in place temporarily before finishing. There is a sculling notch in the crown of the transom.

Next, cut curves in the side edges of the floor panel so that they conform with the edges of the broadstrake (the plank next to the garboard). On the larger canoes, as mentioned, I make the floor narrower—only as wide as the garboards. To trace the curves for cutting, use a tape to measure the width of the canoe bottom at what will be the forward edge of the panel; at what will be the panel's centerline (4 inches aft of the center of the boat); and at the panel's after edge. Transfer these distances onto the floor panel grid, connect these marks with a flexible batten, and draw the curve. After cutting and planing curves on both edges, the floor panel should fit the curves of the broadstrake.

Position the floor and press it down so it lies flat against the planks and keelson. Notice the triangular voids that appear beneath the floor on either side of the keelson. You must fill these voids with floor timbers. With the plywood panel pressed into position, measure and note the distance from the edge of the keelson to the point where the floor touches the garboard. This is the width of the wedge-shaped floor timbers and should be uniform along their length. Red cedar or spruce clapboards can be made to fit these triangular voids, or you can make your own floor timbers by resawing a piece of stock at an angle.

Once the timbers are cut, position them in the canoe, either side of the keelson, then reposition the floor, making sure it's centered. Press down, and mark an outline of the floor all the way around. This outline serves as a boundary, showing you where to spread glue.

Gluing the Floors. Remove the floor timbers and plywood flooring, and apply generous amounts of glue to all surfaces. Position the timbers and again reposition the panel, and nail the floor in place with 3/4-inch ring nails through the plywood and into the center of the keelson, spacing the nails about 4 inches apart. The nails hold the plywood floor down at the center while the glue is drying. A few other pieces of wood push down the rest of the flooring.

After applying glue to the canoe bottom, place floor timbers alongside the keelson.

Take three pieces of scrap 1 x 4, and space them evenly across the rails over the floor. Clamp these pieces to the gunwales with C-clamps. Cut four 3/4-inch-square battens the length of the floor panel and place them on the panel, directly over the feather edges of the timbers and over the seam on either side where the garboards and broadstrakes meet.

Measure the distance from the tops of the battens to the undersides of the 1 x 4s, then add about 3/8 inch. Cut 12 additional batten pieces of this length, and spring these pieces upright between the lengthwise battens and the 1 x 4s. Force them in tightly; they push the floor down, and hold it fast while the glue dries. Once they're in, clean off any excess glue.

After the glue has dried, release the sticks and plane along the lengthwise edges of the floor panel, beveling enough to expose the joints between the panel and the broad-strakes. I like to be able to see these joints so that, in the unlikely event that a leak develops, I can find and fix it easily. Fill the tiny voids at the ends of the panel where the broadstrakes lap the garboards with microballoons and epoxy.

Final Sanding and Shaping

Plane the rail tops smooth, sand the hull interior and rails, and shape and sand the breasthook tops. Chamfer and round off any sharp, square edges with a spokeshave, trimming plane or block plane, and sandpaper. Finish tends to "hang on" to rounded edges better than to sharp, square edges. Fill voids with microballoon putty before sanding so that you won't have to resand.

Carefully position plywood flooring.

Thwarts

For my solo canoes, I make a thwart by first rough-cutting a piece of 1½-inch stock to a length about 1 inch greater than the boat's maximum beam. I want to be sure this crosspiece is long enough at the start to allow me room to cut. Then I measure to its exact midpoint and draw a perpendicular line with a combination square. I'll space the back rests so the edge of each is about ½ inch from this centerline.

I cut the back rests out of ⅜-inch-thick stock. They will be about 9 inches long and 3 inches wide. The shape and dimensions of the back rests are personal choices, however; make them fit your back comfortably. Once they're cut, glue and clamp them to the thwart.

Press the plywood panel down with battens and scrap wood clamped to the rails.

While you're waiting for the back rests to dry, you can make the blocks. The thwart ends swivel inside these pieces, which are mounted on either side beneath the rails. Cut the blocks from a full piece of 1- by 3- by 8-inch stock. The hole in the block should be slightly larger than the coupling on the end of the thwart. The shoulder on the back side can be cut with a router or carved with a chisel; its depth should not exceed 1/2 inch.

For solo canoes, I place the thwarts 14 inches aft of center. Lay a board across the boat at that location, and measure the width of the hull between the insides of the sheerplanks. Divide this distance in half to get the distance to measure out from the center of the thwart—first in one direction, then the other. With a combination square, mark the ends of the thwart and cut them off.

Next, finish off the ends of the thwart with copper. Buy a 1-inch-diameter copper coupling from a hardware store, cut it into two 1-inch-long pieces with either a hacksaw or a pipe cutter, then smooth off the rough edges with a file. Place a 1-inch coupling on the end of the thwart crosspiece, and draw the inside diameter of the coupling on the end grain. Repeat at the opposite end.

Place the thwart in a vise at about a 45-degree angle, and with a spokeshave, eight-side

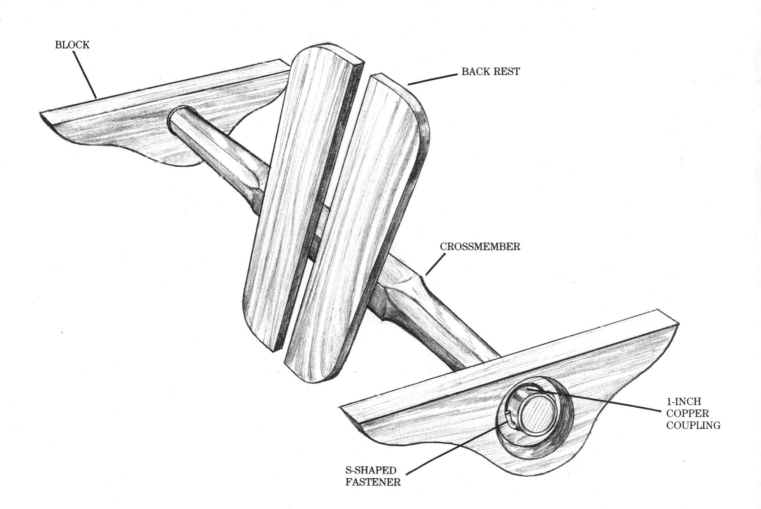

Thwart for a solo canoe.

it from the edges of the back rest to the ends. I do this by eye. Each of the eight sides should stop just shy of being tangent to the 1-inch-diameter circle on the end grain. Round the last inch of the ends with sandpaper, and force the couplings over the ends. Slip the blocks on, drill a hole 1/8 inch in from the end of the copper coupling, and insert a copper rivet or brass rod (equivalent in diameter to a 16-penny nail). Bend it in an S shape so that it can't fall out. This pin holds the thwart in the blocks.

Though the pin may not seem significant, it is. You must have something that ties the sides of the hull together, and those little pins do the job. Attach the blocks to the bottoms of the inwales with two copper rivets or machine bolts per block. *But don't install the thwart until after painting the inside of the hull.*

For larger canoes, I order premade caned seats (see Appendix C, page 127), and fasten them level and beneath the rails.

Use a spokeshave to shape the eight-sided thwart.

9

Spars, Rudders, and Tillers

For small sailing boats, there are numerous choices of rigs. Here, I'll describe the way I make spars for the Flapjack, a 14-foot sailing skiff with a sprit rig. Good boat plans accurately describe and illustrate appropriate rigging.

When making masts or sprits, I prefer northern white spruce because it's available here in Vermont. Sitka spruce is one of the best woods, but it's expensive. I try to buy clear, straight-grain spruce, free of checks. Small pin knots are acceptable if they're sound. To select spar wood, I sometimes spend hours searching through lumberyards.

To shape a piece, or laminated pieces, of square stock into a tapered, round mast or sprit, I use various hand tools, including drawknives, planes, spokeshaves, and a spar gauge.

I finish spars with varnish so that I can see if they're holding up well. Rot beneath hardware can be a problem, but with varnish, you can detect it well before it becomes serious. In keeping with an old schooner tradition, I sometimes paint the spar tips.

From lofting, I make patterns for the rudder and tiller, then trace these shapes onto 3/4-inch mahogany planks. Other acceptable woods include plywood or spruce for a skiff such as the Whisp that is meant to be cartopped. A tiller, which can be derived from your plans, should feel good in your hand. Tillers often have extensions to allow you to hike out or sit amidships.

Spars

Laminating. Whether you're making a mast or a sprit, laminating requires identical steps. For the Flapjack, however, only the mast need be laminated.

Some small-boat designers purposely specify mast or sprit dimensions that enable you to use lumber of widely available dimensions, such as framing lumber like 2 x 6s or 2 x 8s. The Flapjack's mast can be laminated from two pieces of 1 1/2-inch-thick northern white spruce. Rough stock should always be 1/4 inch wider than the intended mast diameter, to allow for planing after the glue-up.

Once I have rough lumber on hand, I glue and clamp the two long pieces together. If you're short on clamps and want to distribute the pressure evenly, screw the clamps down on the center of 6- or 8-inch battens, placed widthwise on the lumber. Space the clamps on 6-inch centers on alternating sides of the wood.

The wood should be straight. To check for bends, run a string down the edge and sight along it carefully. Adjust the spar with weights as necessary to straighten it while the glue dries.

Once the glue dries, remove the clamps and plane the wood to the correct mast diameter, which for the Flapjack is 2 1/2 inches. If you don't have a power planer, do this by hand with a joiner plane or ask a lumberyard to do it for you.

ameter of the snotter line so that the line will slide easily. Begin by drilling a hole 2 inches in from the end, then saw out the sides of the slot. Smooth the inside curve with a rasp or sandpaper.

Later, after shaping the sprit, I drill a hole through the side of, and about ½ inch above the inner end of, the forked slot. Here I insert a rivet to keep the slot from splitting at its apex.

Tapering. Spars are usually tapered, with the narrowest dimensions at either end. By tapering a mast or sprit, you reduce its weight, but retain thickness at the point where stress under sail is greatest.

For example, the Flapjack sprit tapers to a thickness of 1 inch at the ends. So, you must find the center of the end grain and mark a 1-inch-diameter circle. To do this, mark diagonals on the end grain between opposite corners, creating an *X*. The lines intersect at the center. Adjust your compass to ½ inch and draw the circle.

You now have a circle on your end grain, but before you can round the ends you must taper or reduce them to 1-inch squares from the untapered thickness of 1½ inches. The object is to reduce the wood by ¼ inch on each side, at both ends.

With a combination square, make a center mark at the exact longitudinal midpoint of the sprit, and square this all the way around. Refer to your plans, and draw the proper taper on one side, from the edge at the midpoint to a mark ¼ inch in from the edge at the ends. Saw out and then plane the taper, then turn the wood over, and repeat these steps.

If you're planing northern white spruce, long, curling, blond shavings will fall to the floor. I love this wood. The only thing I dislike is its softness. You have only to look at it and it dents.

Mast Halyard Hole. After tapering the mast, you will need to drill a bee hole at the top for the halyard. Usually, I place the hole about 2 inches down from the top and make it

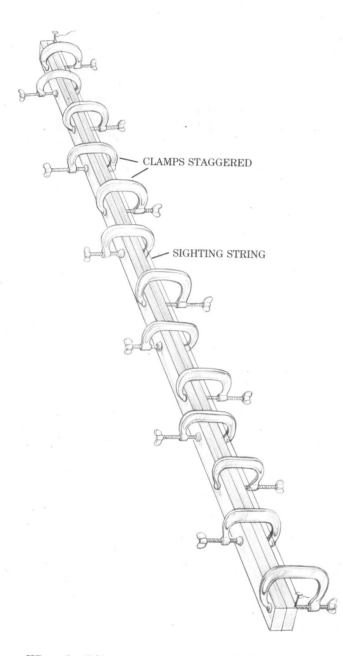

CLAMPS STAGGERED

SIGHTING STRING

When building a spar, use a sighting string to ensure that the boards lie straight for lamination.

Sprit Fork. If you're building a Flapjack sprit, you must next cut a slot into one end of the wood. This 2-inch-long slot accommodates the snotter, a line which tightens the sprit and peaks up the sail (see page 121).

Make the slot slightly wider than the di-

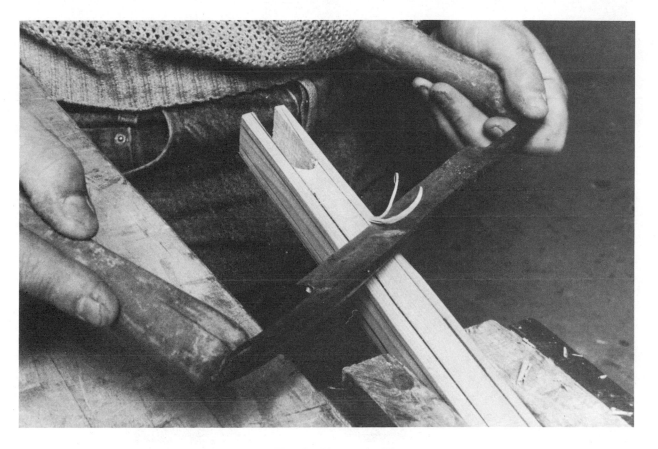

Cut a 2-inch-long fork at the end of Flapjack's sprit. This sprit has also been marked for shaping with a drawknife.

slightly larger than the halyard. For example, if I plan to use a ¼-inch halyard, I'll drill a ³/₈ inch diameter hole. With the mast installed, the hole's openings face fore and aft.

Sprit Peg. After tapering the sprit, whittle a small dowel-shaped peg on the end opposite the fork. In a sprit rig, this peg holds up the peak of the sail. For the Flapjack, the peg is ½ inch in diameter and ¾ inch long. Whatever the boat, it should be small enough so that a sail's roped eye slips over it, but large enough so that it doesn't break off easily.

To carve the peg, measure in ¾ inch from the end of the sprit and make a mark. With your combination square, draw lines or square around the mark, then find the center of the end grain by drawing diagonals on it. When making a peg ½ inch in diameter, set your compass at ¼ inch and draw a circle.

Take a saw (I use my Japanese backsaw) and cut a kerf into the line you squared around the end. Cut just deep enough—all the way around—so that the saw penetrates about as far as the distance to the circumference of the circle on the end grain. Chisel away the wood around the circle, leaving a round, dowel-shaped peg. Smooth with sandpaper.

Spar Gauge. To reduce a mast or sprit from 4 sides to 8, you must have a spar gauge. For small spars, I then do the final shaping—from 8 to 16 sides, and from 16 to round—by eye. A spar gauge is a simple but ingenious tool that allows you to mark a piece of tapered square stock for eight-siding.

For spars up to 3 inches in diameter, I use a 3¼-inch spar gauge made of a piece of hardwood, two nail guides, and two pencils or ballpoint pens. Ballpoint pens make easily seen,

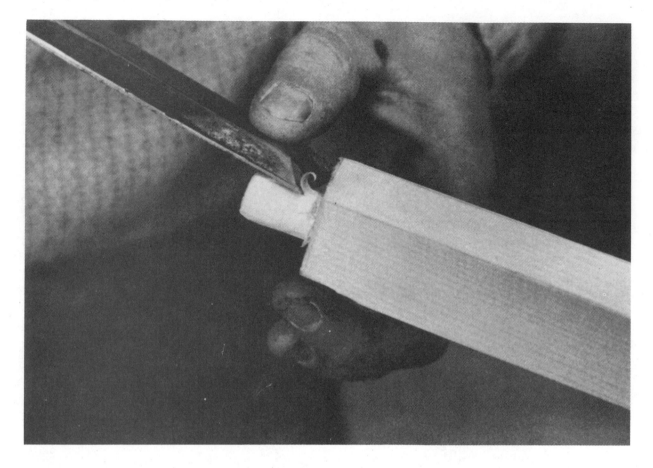

A sprit peg holds up the peak of the sail.

clean, straight lines, while pencils tend to wear down quickly. Some spar gauges scribe lines with nails rather than pens or pencils. To make this gauge, cut a piece of 1-inch-thick stock about 2 inches wide and 6 inches long. Draw a lengthwise centerline; then, from the midpoint of the wood, measure along the centerline $1^5/8$ inches and make a mark. Do the same in the opposite direction. On the outsides of those marks, drill holes for two 16-penny staging nails. These nails, $3^1/4$ inches apart, become the guides.

Now, drill two holes with diameters big enough to hold pens, pencils, or scribing nails snugly, positioning these holes along the centerline, $^{11}/_{16}$ inch from, and on either side of, the midpoint. (This distance is to the center of the holes.) After drilling the holes, insert the pens, pencils, or nails. Then drive in the nail guides.

Starting at the midpoint, hold the gauge

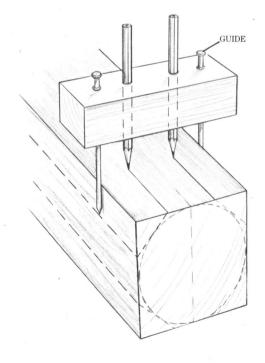

With this gauge, you can mark square stock to be shaped into an eight-sided spar.

Hold the gauge diagonally on your spar, making sure the guides touch the wood.

Shaping a spar with a drawknife makes for quick work. Finer cutting is best done with a plane. Alternatively, use a plane for the entire job.

diagonally on your spar, making sure the guides touch the wood. Slide the gauge along the spar surface, leaving two lines as you go. Hold the guides snugly against the wood all the way. Do this on all four sides, then plane off the square edges, creating flat surfaces between the lines left by the spar gauge. As always, leave your lines. You now have eight sides. I shape the spar from 8 to 16 sides, and from 16 sides to round, by eye. A sense of touch also helps in finding flat spots.

Mast Thumb Cleat. One final detail is the mast thumb cleat, a small, dowel-shaped knob that projects from the mast and supports the snotter loop. At the height indicated on your plan, drill a $3/8$- or $1/4$-inch hole in the mast, then glue and insert a dowel of the same dimension. Leave about $3/8$ inch proud, just enough to catch the snotter. This knob is essential for masts with slick varnish finishes. Often, I install the knob when rigging a boat, after the sail has arrived. To make adjustments easily, lay the whole rig flat on the ground.

Rudders and Tillers

You can loft a rudder directly onto your stock. A Flapjack rudder has pintles on the leading edge that slip into gudgeons attached to the transom. It also has a curved bottom, so that if it goes aground, the rudder pops out of the gudgeons and falls free. A poorly designed rudder won't do this; when it hits bottom, it may rip the gudgeons off and damage the transom.

I make the rudder out of $3/4$-inch-thick mahogany, with a rounded forward edge that has the shape of a $3/4$-inch radius. Taper the rudder from the $3/4$-inch radius straight back to a square trailing edge, $1/8$ inch wide.

Before shaping the rudder, I cast a small amount of lead into a 2-inch-diameter hole in the rudder's forward edge, about $1\frac{1}{2}$ inches from the bottom (see "Casting Lead," page 88).

Final sanding, rounding the eight- or sixteen-sided spar.

This keeps the rudder from floating up out of the gudgeons.

After cutting the rudder blank from mahogany stock, I round the forward edge with a spokeshave so that it becomes bluntly radiused. Then I plane the taper from the radius to the trailing edge.

At the top of the rudder, I glue and screw a 7- to 8-inch block on either side, protruding about 5 inches above the rudder, and sandwich a third 3/4-inch-thick block between the first two at their tops, thus creating a 3/4- by 2-inch mortise for the tiller to slide through. I leave enough room so that the tiller can move up and down, about 1 foot of tiller play at the handle end being desirable. Proper clearance from the transom, so that the tiller won't rub, is also important.

Tiller. I make tillers out of the same wood and of the same thickness as the rudders. Tillers may be scaled off architect's drawings. Attach the tiller to the rudder with a slightly bent pin or a small bolt inserted in a hole drilled through the blocks and tiller. Finish both tiller and rudder by sanding all surfaces.

10
Paint and Varnish

After you've spent several weeks building an ultralight, it makes no sense to skimp on finishes. Sand with increasingly fine papers and apply four to six coats of high-quality marine paint and varnish. For exteriors, I prefer paints because they accentuate the precise lines of lapstrake boats. When painted with light colors, laps create well-defined shadows.

Also, I find paints are easier to apply and maintain than varnishes. In choosing between the two, I remember the workboats of coastal fishermen. In Maine, for example, lobstermen and many wooden-boat builders prefer the practicality of paint over the sheen and high gloss of varnish.

Moreover, sunlight causes exterior varnishes to deteriorate, making frequent refinishing necessary. Burning rays literally cook the finish off a boat. Even varnishes with ultraviolet inhibitors show signs of wear after a few seasons. Some manufacturers claim to have developed improved, long-lasting varnishes with UV inhibitors. The best varnish I've ever used is Z-spar number 1015 Captain's Varnish.

The best time to apply varnish or paint is on a day when the temperature is warm but not excessively hot. Natural outdoor light is better than artificial light, but too much sun and heat will dry your finish too quickly, making it difficult to keep a wet edge; in other words, it becomes difficult to make the finish flow together. Instead, it dries quickly and forms ridges.

Preparation

To prepare a boat for painting or varnishing, I start with 80- or 100-grit 3M production paper and finish with 180- or 220-grit white Tri Mite sandpapers. I wear a dust mask and work outdoors when possible. I have a vacuum on hand to remove dust before applying either paints or varnishes. For initial sanding, I use a 4 x 4 vibrating sander, after which I sand by hand—always working with the grain. For smooth, flat, hand sanding, I use a block backed with stiff rubber, foam, or carpet.

For canoes or small skiffs, I always buy 2-inch-wide foam or sponge brushes. If you use traditional brushes, foam brushes may take some getting used to, but they're perfect for smooth finish work. They never leave brush strokes. Foam brushes are inexpensive; you can simply dispose of them after every coat or after they become soggy. With foam brushes, time-consuming brush maintenance and expensive cleaners are unnecessary. The results are excellent. I keep one or two traditional brushes for tight corners.

Painting and Varnishing

Paint or varnish will last longer if the finish is entirely flat, which means the grain is full. The thicker the finish and the greater the gloss, the longer it will last. A perfectly flat finish, with all the grain filled, has the best chance of reflecting the sun's burning rays. I never use primers, and I thin only when weather requires it. If it's hot and windy, I may add a retarder.

Summarizing, here are the steps to follow when finishing with either paint or varnish:

1. With the 4 x 4 sander and 80-grit or 100-grit paper, smooth all surfaces.

2. Change to 120-grit and resand.

3. Sand again, this time with 180-grit, making sure to remove all scratches.

4. Apply a coat of finish with 2-inch-wide foam brushes.

5. After the finish dries (at least 12 hours, even on a hot day), sand with 220-grit paper.

6. Vacuum.

7. Wipe with a cloth dampened with mineral spirits. This helps clean off the dust film.

8. Wipe with dry cloth. Cotton diapers, cloths, or old sheets work well.

9. Wipe with a tack rag or an antistatic rag, which removes static electricity and picks up any lint or dust on the finish.

10. Apply a second coat of finish.

11. Repeat steps 5 through 10, until you have completed the desired number of coats. I prefer six for a long-lasting finish. Assuming normal use, four coats will produce a finish that lasts about two years, while six are good for four years.

Hardware

After completing all finish work, you can install hardware, such as cleats, pad eyes, seats, mast partner, and mast step. Wherever hardware or fasteners are attached, apply a bedding compound to make them watertight. Dolphinite is a widely used compound that deters rot beneath the hardware.

Epoxy Saturation

While I consider epoxy an excellent material for securing planks and other parts, I rarely use it to cover a boat. Some boat plans

Light colors accentuate the fair lines of a lapstrake hull. (Bruce Beeken photo)

call for epoxy saturation, and in that case I'd follow the designer's instructions. In general, though, I dislike doing this because after I've smeared glue all over a boat, I will then have to sand much of it off to achieve a decent finish. Furthermore, epoxy and oil-based paints appear to react in a way that makes the paints dry and adhere more slowly. Finally, I'm not convinced epoxy offers appreciably more protection than paint alone.

Epoxy, I know from experience, penetrates deeply—perhaps about 1 millimeter. Then it hardens like a rock, making the hulls of 4-mil-limeter plywood canoes brittle. I do not recommend epoxy saturation for these canoes.

Some people believe epoxy applied to plywood prevents checking. Again, I'm not convinced. I have seen a plywood deck covered by epoxy and fiberglass, where the checking split the fiberglass and epoxy. I have also seen a sailboat transom check even after five coats of epoxy.

When it comes to finishes, I'm a traditionalist—I believe in paint for painting and glue for gluing. I don't fasten planks with paint, and I don't paint planks with glue.

Appendix A
Sharpening Tools

When you build a plywood boat, sharp tools are essential. The glue used to laminate plywood dulls tools quickly.

For sharpening plane irons, chisels, and other edge tools, Japanese waterstones are the best and easiest to use. Japanese use them to sharpen samurai swords, perhaps one of the sharpest-edged tools in the world. These waterstones cut metal fast and produce a fine, mirror-like surface with a razor-sharp edge.

For basic sharpening, two stones are all you need. I start with an 800-grit "King Deluxe Coarse Stone" known as a Toishi, which I purchase through the mail from The Japan Woodworker (see Appendix C). The stone measures 8 by 2⅝ by 1⅜ inches. For finishing a sharpening job, I use a "King S-3 Shiage Toishi," which measures 8¼ by 2⅞ by ⅞ inch. Other Japanese waterstones are available in various grits and sizes, ranging in price from about $12 to $300.

Dressing The Stones

One of the beauties of Japanese waterstones is that you can flatten them out, easily removing hollows worn into the center from constant sharpening. Simply rub two waterstones together until the surface is perfectly flat, following your progress with a straightedge.

Alternatively, rub the stone on a piece of sandpaper (220-grit works best) laid on a perfectly flat metal surface such as a tablesaw top. Use a piece of wet or dry sandpaper for this, and with the stone either wet or dry, rub it back and forth over the sandpaper until it is perfectly flat.

A stone with a hollow is absolutely useless for sharpening tools, because the center of the blade edge will not touch the stone, and the corners of the blade will be rounded. When you have trouble getting a sharp edge on a tool, nine times out of ten the stone has a hollow.

Conventional water or oilstones are impossible to flatten by hand. Once a hollow develops in one of these stones, your best course of action is to throw it out.

Always place your stones in water when not in use. I keep mine in a plastic jug with an opening cut out of the top. After a drying period of about two hours, you can actually hear the stone soaking up the water like a sponge. In the winter, my stone sometimes freezes in the jug overnight. This slows me down, but I thaw it out by placing the jug near the woodstove.

Sharpening

If a chisel or plane iron is really dull, I begin sharpening it on a slow-turning grinding wheel. Because the wheel is round, this creates a hollow in the ground face. In other words, if the blade were viewed from the side with its ground surface upward, the profile left by the grinding would be concave. I consider this desirable, because there is subsequently less surface area to work when honing the edge. I then follow up with coarse and finishing waterstones.

To steady the stone and keep it from slipping on your workbench, either place it on a piece of felt or clamp it in a vise. Then lay the beveled edge of the iron as flat as possible on the stone, and starting at the nearest end of the stone surface, push the tool gently toward the other end. Do not try to sharpen on the backstroke. When you have repeated this forward motion for several strokes, you will be able to feel a burr developing on the flat side of the iron.

At this point, you must work on the flat, non-beveled side of the tool to remove the burr. Lay this side of the plane iron or chisel flat on the stone and slide it back and forth. The back side of the iron must be perfectly flat, or the tool won't become sharp.

Remember, these stones cut very fast, and only a few strokes should be required on either side of the tool. Don't try to oversharpen, because too many strokes will remove the hollow in the iron's upper face. When that hollow does disappear, as it will sooner or later, I use the wheel to replace it.

Be sure to keep water on the stone at all times, because it helps form a "paste" or residue on the stone, and the paste aids the sharpening action.

To make a plane work as effectively as possible, make sure the plane itself has a perfectly flat bottom surface. Use a straightedge to check this, and if necessary, with the plane iron removed, place the plane on the stone and push it back and forth to flatten this surface.

A properly sharpened plane iron or chisel should shave hair off a forearm. You can judge an edge by looking at it straight on. If it's dull, you will be able to see some shine on the edge; if it's sharp, it will be invisible.

Appendix B
Ultralight Boats —
A Gallery of Designs

In the canoes I build, you'll see the influence of J. Henry Rushton, a pioneer boatbuilder from the Adirondack region. His turn-of-the-century guideboats, canoes, and skiffs, with their classic lines and furniture-quality finish, set high standards for other builders. I've spent hours studying Rushton's finely crafted boats. He was probably the first ultralight-canoe builder, and his plank-on-frame canoes are lighter than mine made of 4-millimeter mahogany plywood. His 9-foot Sairy Gamp weighed only 9½ pounds. I'm convinced that if he had had plywood and epoxy, he would have built boats with these materials.

Among those who followed Rushton's designs was a canoe builder I worked for, Carl Bausch of Charlotte, Vermont. He took Rushton's designs one step further—using new-age materials and developing innovative ways of building lightweight canoes. Carl rarely used hardwood and never added inwales, making his canoes even lighter than mine. I also learned techniques from Edwin Sturges, of Charlotte, Vermont, who builds wood-canvas canoes. Ed compelled me to make my canoes a little stronger and therefore a little heavier.

Steve Redmond of Burlington, Vermont, has designed most of the glued plywood lapstrake skiffs I've built to date. He designs lightweight, high performance sailing, rowing, and powered craft. I've learned a lot from Steve, a first-rate designer who draws pretty boats. Whisp, Tetra, Flapjack, Bluegill, and Bullhead are all his designs.

Here's a sampling of my favorite ultralight boats. If you decide to build one and would like to purchase complete plans, you'll find addresses for ordering plans in Appendix C.

Charlotte

Length: 11 feet, 6 inches
Depth Amidships: 12 inches
Beam: 27 inches
Weight: 25 pounds

The design influence for this canoe was Rushton's classic Wee Lassie. This is the most popular canoe I build. A finely made, spoon-bladed double paddle can make this little craft really fly.

She is an unusually enjoyable solo boat, offering the exhilarating experience of personal freedom so necessary to the lone paddler. She has enough additional capacity for two or three weeks' gear. The perfect choice for gliding silently over a clear mountain lake.

Charlotte

Daisy May

Length: 13 feet, 10 inches
Depth Amidships: 12 inches
Beam: 33 inches
Weight: 44 pounds

In concept and design, this 13½-foot canoe is similar to the smaller Charlotte. A solo canoeist using a double paddle can handle her without awkwardness because she's still fairly narrow—33 inches amidships. Because the Daisy May has more length and beam than the Charlotte, she also accommodates two paddlers comfortably.

Even though I've slightly crowded the canoe's two seats amidships, there's still plenty of room for two people along with a week's gear. With the canoe turned around, a solo paddler in the bow seat can double-paddle comfortably. The bow does not lift up high out of the water. The seating in this canoe puts weight where it belongs—amidships.

Although the Daisy May measures 13 feet 10 inches, she weighs only 44 pounds. For portaging, I make the center thwart yoke-shaped. Other canoes, such as the Charlotte, may be supported with a strap lashed around the center thwart and threaded between the spaces in the inwales.

Daisy May

Cavendish

Length: 15 feet, 11 inches
Depth Amidships: 13 inches
Beam: 36 inches
Weight: 49½ pounds

At 16 feet and 50 pounds, this is my biggest canoe. I don't recommend larger canoes, because they're difficult to handle easily and quickly. No canoe should require drudgery or anguish. If it does, it won't be used.

The Cavendish has the displacement, stability, and length to take a heavy load safely, making it ideal for family outings and long trips. Its stability increases with load. The Cavendish performs best with three people aboard or two people and a load.

The Cavendish has a shallow V-section hull, a helpful feature when you are traversing an open lake or bay. With pronounced forward flare, this canoe stays dry and tracks well.

Cavendish

Whisp

Length: 15 feet, 9 inches
Beam: 3 feet, 6 inches
Weight: 68 pounds

Whisp is an ultralight sharpie skiff, designed for maximum rowing and sailing performance in a boat that can be cartopped and portaged easily. She's capable of handling 600

Whisp

pounds and is equipped with three caned seats.

She borrows many features from canoe design, and combines these with a flat-bottomed transom-stern hull form to produce maximum stability. She is capable of exhilarating planing performance under sail.

As a rowing boat, she has excellent direc-

tional stability in a crosswind and has proved that she can cover a mile in under 12 minutes with ordinary oars and without a sliding seat. Equipped with an electric trolling motor, she will move steadily at close to 5 miles per hour. A deep-cycle battery will allow you to troll or cruise all day on a single charge.

Whisp

Tetra

Length: 9 feet, 8 inches
Beam: 3 feet, 6 inches
Weight: 60 to 90 pounds, depending
    on scantlings

Around the turn of the century, and even before, coastal New England boatsmen built thousands of wooden skiffs and dinghies. A few years ago, a man named John Dupy came to me with one of these classics. He liked the small boat so much he asked me if I'd build him a new one from scratch.

Duplicating the original meant taking lines off an old rotting hull and developing new plans—too time-consuming a task. So I took the basic dimensions from the Massachusetts dinghy and gave them to designer Steve Redmond. Steve created a new 10-footer called Tetra. She's pleasant to row or sail and makes a perfect small tender.

Both Tetra and Whisp may be built as ultralights or more substantial boats with heavier scantlings. Even with heavier scantlings, which increase the Tetra's weight to about 90 pounds, she's a responsive boat under oar or sail. Tetra's load capacity is about 400 pounds.

Tetra is an efficient boat to build because her bottom is 8 feet long, the exact dimension of plywood sheets. I often use this boat as a teaching tool during my summer courses. Building Tetra could form the core of a high-school shop program, or parents might consider buying plans and sharing an enjoyable winter project with their daughters or sons.

Tetra (Bruce Beeken photo)

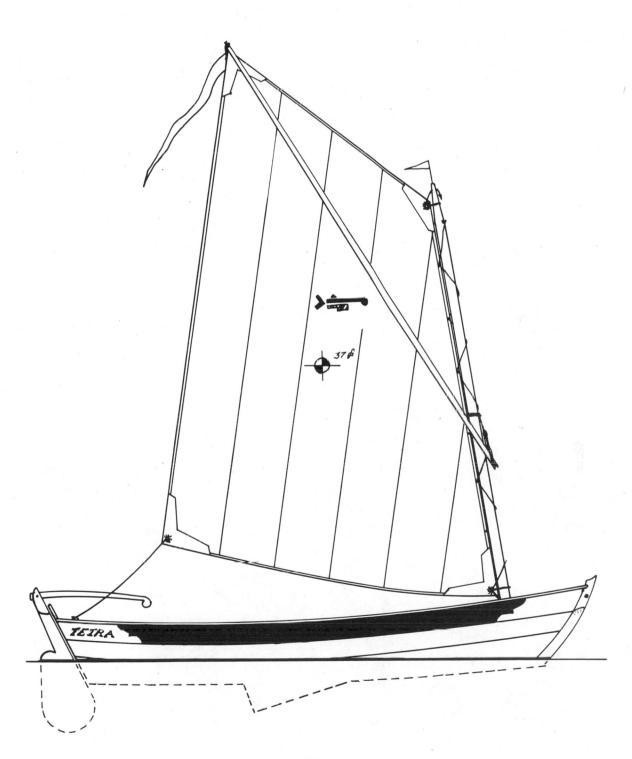

Tetra

Flapjack

Length: 13 feet, 10 inches
Beam: 4 feet, 6 inches
Weight: approximately 120 pounds

Flapjack is the prettiest of all the Redmond skiffs. She's a beautifully proportioned, seaworthy, 14-foot skiff with a sprit rig. This is a great family boat, comfortably accommodating three adults, or two adults and two children. She will plane under sail on a broad reach or a run. Even though she's not a cartopper, Flapjack will fit in the back of a small pickup. When you are rowing with a passenger, Flapjack's seat arrangement allows for excellent trim.

Flapjack

Bullhead

Length: 16 feet
Beam: 7 feet, 11 inches

Bullhead is a 16-foot ultralight catboat with a gunter rig. She has a flat bottom and round topsides. Bullhead has a roomy cockpit, with a small galley and sitting headroom. She will sleep two in a large double berth, making her a good boat for weekend cruises. She can be trailered and beached easily. She's also designed for auxiliary outboard power.

Bullhead

Bluegill

Length: 15 feet, 4 inches
Beam: 4 feet, 9 inches
Weight: approximately 200 pounds

Bluegill is perhaps the easiest of all the Redmond skiffs to build. She has just one plank per side and does not require a building jig to be assembled. Bluegill takes up to a 15-horsepower outboard engine. She has a gunter rig. The largest of the Redmond skiffs, she's extremely stable and can easily accommodate two or three adults.

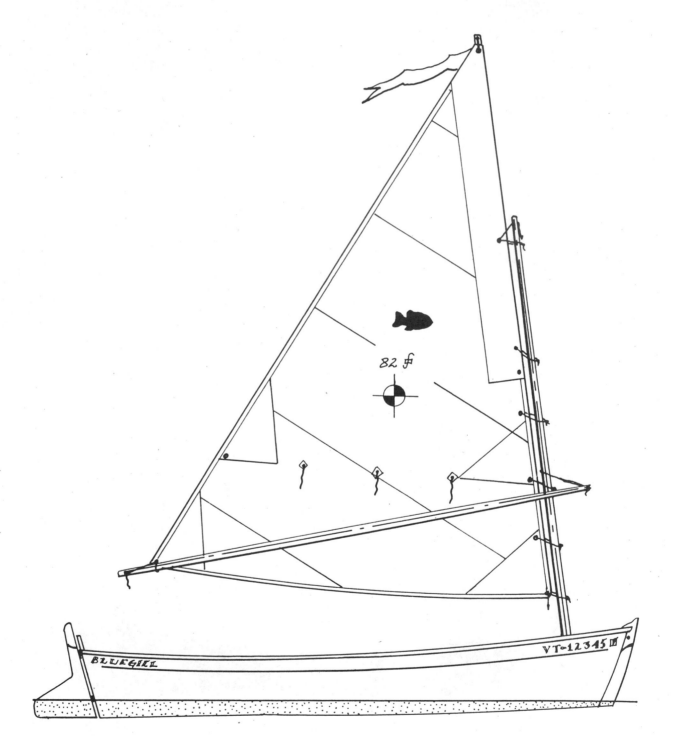

Bluegill

Shearwater

Length: 16 feet
Beam: 4 feet, 5 inches
Weight: 150 pounds

I built this boat in the summer of 1987 with my students at the WoodenBoat School. She's lovely. I've borrowed *WoodenBoat* magazine's description of her, with their kind permission. Her plans can be obtained from *WoodenBoat*:

Another in the series of lapstrake plywood small craft designed by Joel White especially for *WoodenBoat*, Shearwater combines the style of the wonderful open boats of western Norway and the performance of a Maine

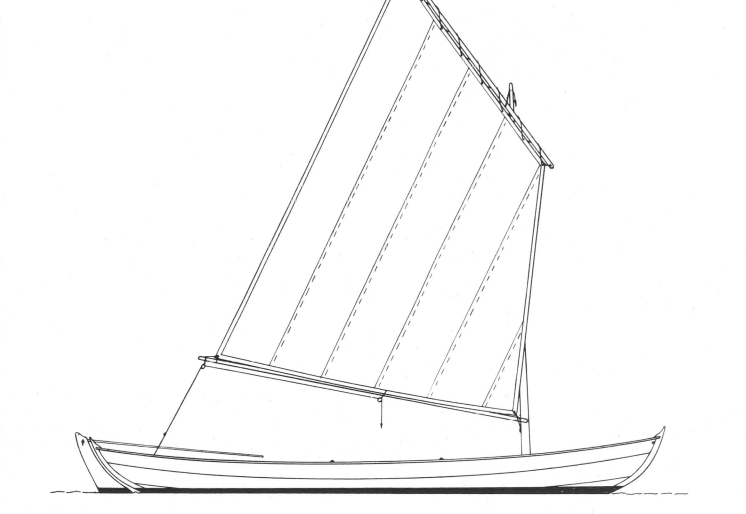

Shearwater

peapod with the ease of construction and durability of lapstrake plywood. She's narrow at the waterline, for a long, lean shape below that lets her glide through the water without fuss; yet, her topsides flare out to give lots of reserve stability and enough beam at the rail so that long oars can be used. Underwater, her bow and stern rise up so that she'll turn quite quickly under oars, and not trip on her forefoot to become a liability when towed as a tender behind a larger boat in a following sea.

Her hull, elegant and shapely as it is, is a study in simplicity, consisting of a backbone, three frames, and six planks—three to a side. We've found her to be unusually fast under sail and great fun in moderate seas, but because of her speed under sail, her low freeboard, and undecked hull, she's not a sailboat for all weather. When it gets rough, she's drier and safer under oars at speeds slow enough for her to rise to meet the oncoming waves.

At 16 feet overall and 150 pounds, she's suitable for cartopping and, at the same time, suitable for carrying a sizeable load. Because she's of plywood, she won't dry out in the sun when not waterborne. And because her interior is uncluttered with the usual frames, chines, seat risers, and inwales, she's very easy to keep clean, to sand, and to paint. Her seats and floorboards are easily removed—they just lift out—making the task of caring for her even easier. There's no doubt about it, Shearwater is a wonderful combination of beauty, simplicity, versatility, and performance.

Plans come in eight sheets, and include sail plan, profile and oars plan, building jig details, construction plan, lines and offsets, plus three sheets of full-size patterns. WB Plan No. 58. $75.00.

Appendix C
Sources

Canoe Plans
Thomas J. Hill
RR 594-16
Huntington, Vermont 05462

Skiff Plans
Redmond Designs
P.O. Box 1605
Burlington, Vermont 05402-1605

Boat Plans
WoodenBoat
P.O. Box 78
Brooklin, Maine 04616

Epoxy
Gougeon Brothers
P.O. Box X908
Bay City, Michigan 48707

Hudson Marine Plywood Co.
P.O. Box 1184
Elkhart, IN 46515

Marine Plywood
Higgins International
1399 Ygnacia Valley Road
P.O. Drawer HL
Walnut Creek, California 94598

Fasteners, Paints, Hand Tools, Adhesives, Varnishes
Jamestown Distributors
28 Narragansett Avenue
P.O. Box 348
Jamestown, Rhode Island 02835

Hand and Power Tools
Woodcraft Supply Corp.
41 Atlantic Avenue
Box 4000
Woburn, Massachusetts 01888

Japanese Hand Tools
Japan Woodworker
1731 Clement Avenue
Alameda, California 94501

Small Brass Bevel Gauge
Walter J. Simmons
Duck Trap Woodworking
P.O. Box 88
Lincolnville Beach, Maine 04849

Sails
Center Harbor Sails and Rigging
Naskeag Road
Box 32
Brooklin, Maine 04616

Paddles, Oars, Canoe Seats
Shaw and Tenney
20 Water Street
Orono, Maine 04473

Xynol and Dynel Cloth
Defender Industries, Inc.
255 Main Street
New Rochelle, New York 10801

Glossary

Aft Perpendicular. The aftmost perpendicular line on a lofting grid. Often referred to as AP.

Backbone. A longitudinal strip of wood that fastens station molds together and at right angles to a canoe jig's strongback. On a skiff jig, a temporary backbone is sometimes used.

Baseline. The horizontal line at the bottom of a lofting grid. To plot the heights of a hull in profile view, you measure up from the baseline.

Batten. A long square piece of knot-free wood used for connecting plotted points when lofting a boat. Also used for "sandwiching" planks to the ribbands during gluing.

Bead. A rim or molding made on the rails with a beading tool.

Belaying Pin. Usually a turned, wooden, dowel-like piece that serves as a cleat for fastening lines.

Bevel. To cut or shape an angle on the edge of a plank or piece of stock.

Breasthook. The structural piece that joins planking together at the stem along the sheer.

Broadstrake. The plank next to the garboard.

Chamfer. A beveled edge.

Chine. I use the term chine to refer to a longitudinal strip of wood that joins the bottom and topsides of a flat-bottomed skiff. Also known as a chine log. Chine commonly refers to the line where the bottom and side meet.

Cleat. A piece of wood used as an additional surface for attaching another piece. Also a T-shaped piece of hardware for fastening lines.

Fair. Without kinks or flat spots. The term fair is also used as a verb, as in fairing hull sides or sheerlines.

False Transom. A piece of wood attached to the transom profiles of a building jig. During planking, the false transom provides backing and support for the boat's transom.

Forward Perpendicular. The forwardmost perpendicular line on a lofting grid. Often referred to as the FP.

Frame. A transverse or vertical structural member that stiffens the hull.

Gain. The joint cut in planking stock to make a hood end flush at the stem or transom.

Garboard. A plank that attaches to the keel or keelson.

128

Grid. Horizontal and perpendicular lines make up the lofting grid, which is used for plotting the curves of a hull.

Gunwale. The longitudinal strip of wood that runs along the hull at the sheer from bow to stern.

Gusset. Usually a plywood triangle used to strengthen right angles of framing members.

Half-Breadth. A view of a boat showing one-half of the hull, as seen from above. Also known as a plan view.

Hood End. The extreme end of a plank.

Inwale. A longitudinal strip of wood fastening at the sheer inside the hull.

Joinery. The process of joining together two blocks or pieces of wood with glue.

Keelson. A strip of wood that runs down the center on the inside of the boat bottom.

Lapstrake. A method of planking a hull, in which each plank or strake slightly overlaps the one below it, giving the appearance of clapboards.

Lining Off. The process of attaching ribbands to station molds in order to determine the number, position, and shapes of the planks on a boat.

Load Waterline. A line representing how deep a boat sits in the water when displaced to its designed load.

Lofting. The process of expanding a naval architect's scale drawing to full scale.

Mast Partner. A transverse piece that holds the mast in position in the bow at the rails.

Mast Step. A block that holds the bottom end of the mast at the floor.

Microballoons. A reddish-brown, powderlike substance mixed with epoxy to make a putty.

Monocoque. A type of construction, often used in building aircraft, in which the outer skin carries all or a major part of the stresses.

Nest. To arrange plank shapes compactly on a plywood sheet in order to minimize waste.

Outer Stem. The forwardmost part of a two-piece stem assembly; sometimes called a cutwater.

Outwale. A longitudinal strip of wood fastening at the sheer outside the hull, also known as the gunwale or guardrail.

Perpendiculars. The vertical lines on a lofting grid, also called station lines.

Profile View. The view of a hull from the side.

Quarter Knee. The structural piece that joins the transom and planking at the sheer.

Ribband. A longitudinal batten used in a building jig

Rocker. The curve of the bottom of the boat.

Scarf. To glue two beveled pieces of wood together end-to-end in an overlapping but flush manner.

Sheer. The uppermost line in a profile view of the boat's hull.

Sheerstrake. The uppermost plank.

Skeg. The vertical, aftermost piece of the keel of a boat. A skeg increases directional stability.

Snotter. The line that attaches the sprit to the mast.

Spacer Pad. A small block of wood, the thickness of the planking, placed between the panel and ribband when spiling.

Spar. The timbers used to fly sails.

Spar Gauge. A tool for marking a spar when reducing it from four to eight sides or more.

Spiling. A term used to denote the process of transferring plank shapes from a building jig to the plank stock, or marking a curved piece of wood to get it to fit another curved piece.

Spreader. The piece that forces apart the two longitudinal members of a jig's strongback.

Sprit. The spar that peaks up a sail on a sprit rig.

Sprit Fork. The fork on the forward, lower end of a sprit that allows the snotter to attach to the sprit.

Station Mold. The cross-sectional piece of a building jig.

Stem. The timber to which planks attach in the forwardmost part of the boat.

Stem Profile. A profile view that includes the area from the aftermost part of the stem aft to the first station line.

Strongback. Usually two longitudinal pieces of lumber that support the station molds of a building jig.

Thwart. A structural transverse piece sometimes used as seating or for carrying canoes.

Transom. The transverse planking forming the stern of a square-ended boat.

Transom Crown. The curve of a transom above the sheerline.

Transom Profile. A profile view that includes the area between the aftmost station and the transom.

Ultralight Boat. An unusually light boat, planked with high-grade, durable, mahogany plywood and glued together with high-performance epoxy.

Waterlines. Horizontal lines that run parallel to the base of a lofting grid in profile view.

Index